HOW DIFFERENT ARE PEOPLE
WHO ATTENDED LUTHERAN SCHOOLS

HOW DIFFERENT
ARE PEOPLE
WHO ATTENDED
LUTHERAN SCHOOLS

MILO BREKKE

Concordia Publishing House, St. Louis, Missouri
Concordia Publishing House Ltd., London, E. C. 1
© 1974 by Concordia Publishing House

ISBN 0-570-01512-X

Contents

Foreword

In my review of this study I have indicated differences with the author on how survey analysis ought to proceed. These differences, however, do not diminish my conviction that the findings of the report are important and impressive. Lutheran parochial schools do have an impact, and that impact is especially impressive when a person has spent a substantial amount of time (12 years optimally) in such a school.

There was a time, of course, when such a finding was taken for granted. Everyone knew that parochial schools worked, and it made sense that these schools had a cumulative impact on their students. But all that has now changed. For the past two decades parochial schools have been on the defensive, and the assumption that they *do not* have any impact has risen to the status of an unquestioned and unquestionable dogma. So unquestionable has this assumption become that it is now almost impervious even to contrary empirical findings.

Over a decade ago in our study of Roman Catholic parochial schools, Peter Rossi and I arrived at conclusions similar to the above. Both the critics and the supporters of Catholic schools, however, were firmly convinced that our findings were the opposite of what in fact they were. From the first *New York Times* article about "The Education of Catholic Americans" to the present, the popular image of our study has been that it proved Catholic schools didn't work. Even today I am occasionally asked why I wrote "that book against Catholic schools."

Sometimes I think you can't win.

Since "The Education of Catholic Americans" was published, there have been a number of replications of its findings — most recently by Edward Cleary in a study of parochial schooling in Peru, and now by the present report. I am always edified and encouraged by such replications; they prove that the work we did in 1963 was not all that bad. But our 1963 study is still misunderstood. For example, in his book, *Coping,* my good friend, the Ambassador to India, cites the Greeley-Rossi report as one in a series of studies which show that parochial schools have little impact on the behavior of students. As I have said, sometimes you can't win.

There will be, I think, three principal reactions within the Lutheran community to the present book:

1. It will be widely assumed that the book proves that parochial schools do not make a difference in the adult behavior of those who attended them. Mind you, the findings of the book are just the opposite; still this assumption will become widespread and ultimately unassailable.

2. A minority group will concede that the findings show an impact of parochial school education; but either the validity of the findings will be denied, or their size and importance will be minimized.

3. A third group will probably ask: What difference does it make if the schools have an impact on those who attended them? What about those who did not attend? The implication is that the church should give up a moderately effective educational technique because it hasn't reached everyone. The substitute for parochial schools should be some unproven educational technique which may (or may not) reach everyone. Two birds in the bush are worth a bird in the hand. And why didn't Jesus decamp for Athens or Rome instead of staying, of all places, in Galilee?

I presume it is clear that I think such reactions will be fatuous. On the subject of parochial school education folly is almost *de rigueur.* My colleague, William McCready, and I recently issued a report indicating that on some measures of ultimate world view, those who attended Roman Catholic parochial schools were overwhelmingly different from non-Catholic school products. Naïvely we thought that Catholic educators would be pleased. Instead the bedeviled Catholic education bureaucrats jumped all over us. Things are so bad in the parochial school world that you not only slay the herald who brings bad news, but you also slay the one who brings good news.

How can this be? Why do the rules of sane discourse break down on the subject of parochial schools? There are a number of reasons. The elites in American society have always been against parochial schools and have always been committed to the now badly tarnished myth that the public school is a great Americanizing institution. Those upwardly mobile members of the Lutheran and Catholic communities who aspired to be accepted by the secular elites find that repudiation of parochial schools is an absolutely essential price to pay for such acceptance.

Second, for reasons having to do with the unsettled state of our times, there has been an immense loss of confidence in the "relevance" of religion and in the utility of every kind of pastoral work. It is as though parochial ministers and parochial school teachers no longer have the moral and emotional energy left to believe in anything they do. Pessimism and despair have become the swamp from which they cannot escape and from which they appear not to want to escape.

Finally, for reasons I must leave to psychologists of the abnormal to explain, the school in American society has become an inkblot, a marvelous scapegoat to be blamed for all social ills. The churches, quick to follow the fashions of the secular society, have turned parochial schools into an inkblot to blame for everything that is wrong with the churches. When research reports like the present one suggest that scapegoating may not be valid, those who have an emotional investment in blaming the schools for everything simply cannot yield that investment in the face of such fragile things as factual research findings. Schools *must* have failed; no other possibility can be considered.

We thus have the peculiar situation in which many people associated with parochial schools are obsessed with a passionate desire to disbelieve good news. This report brings good news — moderate good news perhaps — but in the world in which we live, even that is good enough. As a purveyor of good news, I confidently predict that the report will be in trouble. The author should be flattered. I am unaware of any decent social research on a concrete problem in the last two decades that has not been in trouble. Welcome, sir, into the club. Messrs. Coleman, Rossi, Moynihan, and I are happy to have you aboard.

ANDREW M. GREELEY

Preface

I believe this book can stand by itself. However, the possibilities for misunderstanding will be diminished significantly for anyone who has at least a cursory acquaintance with *A Study of Generations,* also prepared by Youth Research Center. This research has grown out of that major work, is based on the same data, and uses the same dimensions and themes. In preparing this report, I faced the choice of either attempting to restate much of what is in *A Study of Generations* or merely to make reference to the most relevant parts and assume the reader's familiarity with them. I chose the latter course of action.

This project would not have been possible without the generous contribution of computer time by Lutheran Brotherhood of Minneapolis, Minnesota. Most other costs were underwritten by a grant from the Clara and Spenser Werner Foundation to the Board of Parish Education of The Lutheran Church—Missouri Synod, which authorized the project. I am grateful to Ralph Underwager for articulation of questions that could be addressed with the data. Ernest Thompson, Vern Suhr, and Dennis Bornes served long careful hours as systems analyst and computer operators. Very important clerical help was provided by Marilyn Graves, Solveig Heintz, Mary Kay O'Brien, Gaylene Grimm, Diane Blosberg, and Joanne George.

Critical comments on design and manuscript from Merton P. Strommen and Arthur L. Johnson, plus editorial assistance from Frederick A. Meyer, greatly improved the entire report.

I am especially grateful for the patience and encouragement of Delbert Schulz and Al Senske, staff members of the Board of Parish Education.

MILO L. BREKKE
Youth Research Center
Minneapolis, Minnesota

CHAPTER ONE

An Unusual Opportunity

Introduction

Last evening I attended midweek Lenten worship. Among the participants were members of a choir from one of our church-related colleges. After they had clearly and magnificently articulated a melodic version of a Scripture portion, our pastor went to the lectern and, in the course of making announcements, made some comments about parochial schools. He stated that, as far as he was concerned, music such as we had just heard must be included among the many distinctive outcomes of parochial education. He referred not only to the content and quality of the music but also to the intense personal involvement of the singers. In fact, he went so far as to say he wondered if this kind of "music in the lives of people," figuratively speaking, could not be identified as an outstanding result of parochial education. Be that as it may, my point is this: Behind statements such as these are the assumptions that parochial schools make a unique impact on their students, that graduates of parochial schools are different from their public school counterparts, and that the difference is positive—something about which to be enthusiastic and elated.

Is that really so? I would guess that the majority of worshipers agreed with the pastor's assumption. But there was undoubtedly a difference of opinion and, in some cases, strong differences of opinion.

How much confidence can be placed in these opinions? The intuitive conclusions of sensitive and experienced people are usually very valuable. Nevertheless, do we have any hard scientific data regarding the effectiveness of parochial schools?

If one examines research literature for first-quality, broad-scale studies concerning effectiveness of parochial schools, the results of that search can be summarized in two words: scarce and inconclusive. There is no paucity of attempts at investigating a variety of possible consequences of parochial education, but there is a definite scarcity of broad-scale studies that have used the best scientific procedures.

During the last decade two studies have received national publicity. Both were reported in 1966. The first was conducted through the National Opinion Research Center by Andrew M. Greeley and Peter H. Rossi. This comprehensive national survey of Roman Catholic education concentrated on four general issues that run through most discussions of the relative merits of public and Catholic schools: (1) Are the people who attend Catholic schools better Catholics by a variety of indicators of what constitutes being a "good" Catholic? (2) Does the Catholic school system set its students apart from other Americans and create barriers to their cooperation with Protestants and Jews? (3) Are Catholic schools competent to prepare a person for life in a secular world where occupational success not only contributes to his general level of economic well-being but also has a significant impact on his general social status? (4) Will Catholic parents continue to increase or even maintain their support?

Though in this author's opinion the findings were generally favorable to Catholic parochial schools, the potentially inconclusive nature of the results was emphasized by this paragraph from the preface of the report:

> Both advocates and critics of Catholic Schools will find much here to support their respective views; consequently, neither side will be entirely happy with the results. As with most controversial issues the reality is much more complex than the rhetoric of the disputants would have us believe. Many will regret that the authors do not come down firmly either for or against the Catholic school system but content themselves with pointing out as clearly as the data will permit, the strengths and weaknesses of the system as it has worked over the past fifty

years. The practical implications of the analysis must be left to the policy-makers and the polemicists.[1]

The second more limited study was conducted from the Concordia Seminary Research Center by Ronald L. Johnstone. Whereas the Greeley and Rossi study was based upon a national random sample of 3,753 Roman Catholics between the ages of 23 and 57, the Johnstone study was based on a sample of 584 Lutheran youth (almost entirely of The Lutheran Church — Missouri Synod) who at the time were enrolled in high schools in St. Louis and Detroit. A wide variety of data was collected from each youth by interview and analyzed in relation to the overall question, "What difference does Lutheran parochial education make in the belief, attitude, and behavior patterns of Lutheran youth?" A second very significant question was addressed by categorizing all students into three groups on the basis of family type: "To what degree does family background and home environment explain differences initially traceable to education?"[2] The results were generally interpreted as not extremely supportive of the effectiveness of Lutheran parochial schools. If one compares the results of these two studies, the findings are inconclusive with regard to the impact of parochial schools in general by comparison with public schools.

Both of the above studies were designed explicitly to investigate the effectiveness of parochial schools, and their data were collected with that distinct purpose in mind. By contrast, the data from which this research is being reported were *not* collected for the purpose of assessing the distinctive effects of parochial schools. As part of a nationwide sample survey, they were collected for the broad purpose of describing the beliefs, values, attitudes, opinions, religious life styles, and environmental settings of Lutherans ages 15 — 65 throughout the continental United States. Nevertheless, the data did include the information necessary to make comparisons between persons who were educated in parochial schools and those who were not. Furthermore, because they were collected for other purposes, these data also made it possible to investigate whether apparent positive effects of parochial school experience might be traceable to a wide variety of other variables such as age and general amount of education that persons finally secured, that might account for differences that do show up in the profiles of those who went to parochial schools in comparison with those who did not. There is then a sense in which the data upon which this research was based are neutral data. They were collected as part of a very large body of descriptive information covering several hundred areas of interest. One of these areas happened to be whether people ever attended a Lutheran parochial school and, if so, for how long and at what grade levels. The possibility in the data of systematic bias for or against parochial education was practically nil since the data were collected before this research was even proposed. Nevertheless, the timing was opportune, for the data were still very fresh.

The Opportunity Afforded By *A Study of Generations*

This study of parochial school education is, therefore, an afterthought or offshoot of *A Study of Generations,* conducted by Youth Research Center and reported in a book of the same name by Merton P. Strommen, Milo L. Brekke, Ralph C. Underwager, and Arthur L. Johnson (Minneapolis: Augsburg Publishing House, 1972). The extreme care with which that national sample survey of Lutherans was conducted is reported in great detail in Appendix A of that book.

Brief Characteristics of A Study of Generations

Three hundred sixteen congregations representative of all of the parishes in the three major Lutheran bodies, The Lutheran Church—Missouri Synod, The Lutheran Church in America, and The American Lutheran Church, were visited in the summer of 1970. These congregations were the 87% that were willing to participate out of a random sample stratified by size of congregation and the nine census regions of the United States. Questionnaires consisting of 740 items were completed by 4,745 persons representing the participating congregations. These

15

4,444 lay people and 301 pastors were the 67% who were willing to participate from a random sample of members, ages 15 – 65, of participating congregations. A follow-up of the randomly selected persons who did *not* take part in the study showed that they were *not* appreciably different from those who did take part. The several million pieces of information were analyzed by very complex mathematical procedures (reported in detail in Appendix A mentioned above). These procedures allowed the data to organize themselves into themes and dimensions that reflected the frames of reference of the people who answered the questionnaires. By summer 1971, some 78 dimensions of belief, value, attitude, opinion, and life style had been isolated. These organized into 14 major themes or factors as reported in the book summarizing the study. Each of these dimensions and factors is a reliable measure of some facet of the lives of Lutherans.

Parochial School Experience Data Available

By spring of 1972 the data bank from *A Study of Generations* that was available for further analysis included scores for every individual on every one of the 78 dimensions as well as the 740 individual questions. Question 720 read as follows:

> What part of your general education below college was from church operated schools (Christian day school, parochial schools)? Mark as many as apply to your attendance, even if you attended only part of the time. If none, leave blank. (a) grades 1 – 3, (b) grades 4 – 6, (c) grades 7 – 9, (d) grades 10 – 12 (or their equivalent).

Information from this question permitted the sample to be separated into subgroups with no parochial school experience by contrast with those reporting varying amounts of attendance at schools operated by the church.

A number of fortunate circumstances converged in an opportunity for additional significant research. First, the entire *A Study of Generations* data bank was already computerized and included norms on all scales and single items not only for Lutherans as a whole but for each of the three Lutheran bodies separately. Second, personnel from Youth Research Center (YRC) who had conducted *A Study of Generations* were available to pursue additional analyses. Third, Lutheran Brotherhood Insurance Company, co-holder of the data together with YRC, had granted additional computer time for research not planned as part of the original study. Fourth, the Board of Parish Education of The Lutheran Church — Missouri Synod expressed interest and authorized a study comparing The Lutheran Church — Missouri Synod members who reported varying degrees of parochial school experience.

The small number of persons reporting parochial school attendance in the other two bodies (The American Lutheran Church and The Lutheran Church in America) discouraged the use of data from parishes other than The Lutheran Church — Missouri Synod. However, of the 1,573 members of The Lutheran Church — Missouri Synod in the sample, 597 reported some attendance in parochial schools during the first 12 years of their education. Table 1.1 shows the 12 patterns of attendance reported by them. Decisions about how to group people by combining various attendance patterns were not made until the questions to be addressed by the study were clearly formulated.

TABLE 1.1

LCMS Patterns of Parochial School Attendance

Pattern of Attendance	Only Grades Attended	Number of Lay People	Number of Clergy
A	1 – 3	57	0
B	1 – 6	26	1
C	1 – 3 and 7 – 9	4	0
D	1 – 9	115	5
E	1 – 6 and 10 – 12	0	2
F	1 – 12	23	22
G	4 – 6	56	2
H	4 – 9	29	2
I	4 – 12	4	7
J	7 – 9	167	1
K	7 – 12	9	8
L	10 – 12	43	14
	Total	533	64

The Focus of the Study

Two characteristics of the available data placed limitations on the issues that could be investigated. Any question had to be ruled out that would require separating the 597 attendees into too many subgroups for reliable comparisons. Even a pool of 740 questions had some limits as to subject matter. However, the following 13 questions could be investigated in considerable detail.

1. *Does attending a parochial school make any difference at all?* Regardless of the number of years attended, regardless of the grades, regardless of when and at what school, is there evidence that people who received some part of their first 12 years of education in a church-related school are different in some *significant* ways? It would seem extremely unlikely that when compared on the basis of more than 700 questions there would be no differences. But if differences are found, do they, for example, form patterns that resemble the objectives of Christian day schools generally held by educators in the church? One might well expect that if the profile of parochial school graduates is different, it should be different in ways that are important. Are the kinds and degrees of difference great enough so that the typical parochial school teacher might say, "Yes, it's well worth it. I'll gladly continue investing my skills and energy in parochial education for years to come?"

2. If attending a parochial school makes a difference, *does more parochial schooling produce greater effects?* If one boy attends for 6 years and another for 12, can we expect the latter to demonstrate even more distinctly those attributes that characterize the 6-year attender? It was when attempting to answer this question that the extremely reliable measuring scales available in *A Study of Generations* data became invaluable. Had rather unreliable measures each based on the information from just a very few questions been the only ones available for making comparisons, this issue could not have been addressed with any reasonable expectation of success. Even with sets of 10, 12, and 15 questions combined into very sensitive and re-

liable measuring scales, it was still audacious but not entirely unreasonable to attempt to find degrees of difference associated with varying amounts of exposure to education in Lutheran day schools. And data were available to isolate both strengths and weaknesses in considerable specificity.

3. *If a person is going to attend only certain grades in a church related school, are some grades better than others?* Greeley and Rossi, for example, found evidence that attendance at a church *college* seemed to have the greatest influence particularly on males. Table 1.1 indicates that there are several common patterns of attendance. Rather large numbers attended only during the junior high school years at about the time of confirmation instruction. Is that better than attending, for example, grades 1−3? Might congregations be better stewards by more fully developing educational offerings either for only a very few carefully selected grades or for certain seemingly more impressionable periods in life?

4. The persons sampled in *A Study of Generations* received the first 12 years of their education at different times over a 60-year span. Thus, a kind of miniature longitudinal study of the possible different effects of parochial education over the years was feasible. References to parochial schools in "the good old days" with the implication that things aren't what they once were, may be nostalgic, but not exactly uncommon. On the other hand, the introduction of new curricula, advances in pedagogy, and the raising of requirements for certification of teachers and administrators is noted. And the claim is sometimes made that one should expect the products of recent parochial school involvement to be superior to those of the past. The large number of people in the sample and information regarding the age of all participants made it possible to investigate the question, "*Does it make a difference when a person got his parochial school education?* Were schools really better in the twenties, the thirties, the fifties?"

5. To find *any* difference can be fascinating, but the ultimate question for many people will be, "*Does going to Lutheran*

schools produce better Lutherans?" or even "good" Lutherans?
Defining what a "good" Lutheran is can be a difficult problem
for any researcher. The fact that the Lutheran Church is a con-
fessional church is a distinct advantage in reaching such a definition. Having neutral data from *A Study of Generations* also
gave additional advantages because norms for all Lutheran
clergy, and particularly pastors of The Lutheran Church—Missouri Synod, were available on all 78 scales and 739 items. Clergy
may not be ideal Lutherans. However, the average score for
clergymen on a variety of measures at least gave a base line
against which to make comparison: when asking if parochial
schools develop in their graduates the value orientations and
beliefs of the Lutheran Church as well as a stronger sense of
attachment to the church. Since most pastors have received
their education in parochial schools, it was necessary to isolate
the effects of parochial school education from "being a clergyman" by comparing average scores for the pastors with average
scores for laymen who were graduates of parochial schools.

Furthermore, the wide variety of dimensions of belief and
value available in *A Study of Generations* made it possible to
avoid attempting any precise definition of what is a good Lutheran. When making interpretations about the development
of "good" Lutherans, it was possible to assume generally that
lower-than-average scores on measures such as salvation by
works, questionable personal activities, disappointment with
the church, generalized prejudice, pessimism, and Biblical
ignorance were desirable. It was also assumed that *higher-than-
average scores* on measures such as Biblical knowledge, belief
in a personal caring God, personal evangelism, neighborliness,
transcendental meaning in life, and personal piety would also
be desirable. Whether the findings are good or bad must become
ultimately the judgment of both the church and each individual
reader of this report.

    6. The charge is sometimes made that those who find an ac-
tive life in the church are dropouts from community life or are the

unsuccessful ones in the larger world. If this is the case, one might expect that those who have grown up in a special educational environment of the church would be especially *inactive* in community life in their adult years. Also, it has been frequently suggested that certain people are no longer interested in the church because they had too much religious experience in their childhood. If that is the case, one might also expect parochial school graduates to be much less active in the church in their later years. It was not possible to check such causal hypotheses. However, plenty of data were available to clearly indicate an answer to the question: *Are those educated in parochial schools more or less involved in church and broad community life than their public or other private school counterparts?*

7. Some social science theorists hypothesize that as people experience more and more of a sense of belonging through their participation in any given group they necessarily develop a set of negative attitudes toward a person who is not part of that group. As in-group feelings develop, definite out-groups must necessarily be identified and, if not ridiculed, at least be rejected, avoided, or treated as inferiors. On the basis of such theorizing, some critics of the church hypothesize that an experience such as many years in the possibly isolated environment of a parochial school might well have divisive effects. Thus, they argue, it would not be unusual to find higher levels of prejudice among those who have been most actively participating in the life of the church and particularly those raised in parochial schools.

In like manner, could there not be this corollary? If a Gospel environment of warmth, acceptance, and mutual love pervades the classrooms of Lutheran schools, could the products of Lutheran schools be much less conscious of social ills? Because so many of their own needs have been met, could they be much less sympathetic to injustices suffered by other people and much more inclined to look the other way when people other than "their kind" are suffering? Whatever the sources out of which it may have grown, *is prejudice one of the fruits of a Christian education received through attending parochial schools?* Or on the positive side, *does life in the environment of the church's day schools do anything to diminish prejudicial and inhumane attitudes toward other people?*

8. *Are those who attend parish schools helped or hindered in coming to grips with the world?* This is more difficult to measure than something like participation in community life or involvement in terms of attendance in various facets of church life. The issue here is whether or not those who have gone to parochial schools have a greater or lesser tendency to withdraw from the full breadth of life's experiences. Do they manifest feelings of isolation, pressure, anxiety, general pessimism, disappointment with work or church? Are they unable to recognize the presence of a loving and caring God in the midst of congregational life? No single item or measure was used to draw conclusions about these questions. Responses to questions such as, "Have you ever gone to a psychologist, psychiatrist, or some other therapist for help with your emotional problems?" or "Indicate the number of close friends (not family or relatives) you have, or people you feel really care about you," were studied in an attempt to determine if parochial education might result in a general isolationism and exclusivism or in a more cosmopolitan, outgoing, caring, reveling in the fullness of life. The configuration of responses to a variety of measures had to be studied very carefully in order to draw conclusions about these differences of worldview that seem so subtle when one is trying to measure them, but that are so overwhelming in their impact.

9. And then what about plain, ordinary, everyday information? *Do people coming out of parochial schools know more about the church and the faith? Do they give evidence of greater clarity in their understanding of the doctrines of the church?* *A Study of Generations* found that generally among Lutherans ignorance of or misinformation about the Bible is significantly related to belief in salvation by works, placing a high value on personal development, and participation in questionable personal behaviors. By contrast, Bible knowledge was found to be

significantly related to belief in Jesus' humanity and to a tendency to apply the Gospel in one's interpersonal relationships.

10. Historically Lutherans have placed great emphasis on the importance of the distinction between Law and Gospel, particularly in preaching and care of souls. In *A Study of Generations* this distinction was found to be far more than academic. The two most salient factors or themes found to run through the configurations of belief, value, attitude, opinion, and behavior among Lutherans contrasted these two ways of life. One of two orientations to life as a whole were found to predominate in the lives of large numbers of Lutherans. The first is an orientation to Gospel: a living in, believing, experiencing and accepting the Gospel of grace, faith, hope, relationship, and forgiveness. The other is predominantly a living under the Law in the sense of structure, need for achievement, authority, right and wrong, and justice. That finding sharpened up the question, *"Is parochial education associated with greater or lesser understanding of the distinction between Law and Gospel? Or even more important, is there a tendency toward increased legalism or greater freedom under the Gospel among those who have gone to parochial schools?"*

11. *Is parochial education associated with greater or lesser frequency of reported acts of Christian service to other people?* The day-to-day graces of life — kindness, sharing, cooperation, going out of one's way to help, sympathy — all take the form of specific words and actions at convenient and inconvenient times. Scales such as Neighborliness; Supporting Others in Crises; Personal Evangelism; Personal Initiative in Church and Public Issues; and The Church, Me, and Social Justice were used to assess this possible outcome of having attended day schools of the church during one's youth. Very contrasting measures were also available. A scale called Questionable Personal Activities was made up of a whole series of questions about the frequency with which persons lied, became drunk, physically fought, participated in illicit sexual activities, and the like. Although it was not anticipated, the possibility was

present in the design of this study for finding parochial education to be associated with destructive, antisocial, and sinful behaviors should that systematically be the case.

12. ʻThe Bible pictures the church as the family of God. Some therefore assume that if a person experiences the concentrated life of the church in a parochial school setting, he should also gain depth of experience and skills in relating to other people as a family. It is also well known that church members have more stable family lives; at least the statistics indicate less divorce among church members than the general population. If people who attend parochial schools are influenced to be better Lutherans and better church members, it should also follow that their family lives should be more stable and happy. With a rationale such as this, and numbers of data somewhat smaller than related to previous questions, we pursued a twelfth question, *"Did those with parochial education report greater or lesser satisfaction with, and stability of, family life?"*

When one recognizes this concern as two questions, some interesting ramifications become apparent. Suppose that our evidence showed that families of persons who are educated in parochial schools appeared to be more stable but less happy? What would be the implications of finding just the opposite?

13. The last question that could clearly be pursued on the basis of *A Study of Generations* data was rather broad. *Is either decreased or increased sense of meaning or purpose-in-life associated with a parochial education?* When we asked this question of the data, we had in mind not only the possibility of the parochially educated having a clearer concept of their destinies as children of God but also whether they sensed deeper meaning in the very daily aspects of life. This question raised issues about self-image, sense of personal worth, and the consequence of one's existence. Joy of living—including a celebration of one's own individuality and the significance of every other person—was contrasted with the conviction that one is just another number, an infinite inconsequence in a galaxy of repetition, duplication, and meaninglessness.

24

In summary, the questions asked regarding persons with varying degrees of formal parochial schooling by contrast with persons who reported no parochial school attendance whatsoever were as follows:

1. Are they different in any way? (Whether or not that difference can be traced to their parochial education.)
2. If so, does more parochial school attendance produce greater effects?
3. Do certain grades have greater or particularly different impact than others? Or are there certain stages in life when children are apparently more impressionable and thus particularly affected by parochial education?
4. Have they been affected very much differently by differences in parochial schools over the past 60 years?
5. Are they better Lutherans?
6. Are they more actively (not deeply) involved in church and community life?
7. Are they less prejudiced and more humane?
8. Are they helped or hindered in coming to grips with the world outside?
9. Do they know more about the Bible?
10. Do they have greater tendencies toward either legalism or freedom in the Gospel?
11. Do they more frequently report acts of personal service to others or behaviors that may be described as weaknesses of the flesh?
12. Do they report greater or less satisfaction with family life and stability of family life?
13. Do they sense greater meaning and purpose in their lives?

In several instances the same data applied to more than one question. Therefore until the concluding chapter of this report, findings are not organized on the basis of these 13 questions but rather in terms of the 78 scales and additional single items. Also the groups of persons contrasted by varying amounts of parochial school attendance are compared with each other and with average scores for both the clergy and laity as a whole.

25

Three Attendance Variables

The 12 patterns of parochial school attendance reported in Table 1.1 obviously provided too many categories with too few people in many of the categories for reliable results. Several criteria were used for reorganizing patterns. First of all, questions 2 and 3 above required two contrasting groupings of the attendance patterns (Does more parochial school attendance produce greater effects? If all grades are not attended, is it better to attend certain specific grades than others?). Second, Table 1.1 clearly showed that certain attendance patterns were much more common than others. This raised the further question of whether certain common patterns are particularly better or worse than others. Therefore three attendance variables were created by reorganizing the 12 patterns: (1) by number of years attended, (2) by which grades were attended, and (3) by the most common attendance patterns.

Number of years attended. The first parochial school attendance variable was formed on the basis of number of years attended regardless of when that attendance occurred (i. e., what chronological years), and also regardless of what grades (e. g., a person who attended grades 1 − 3 only was placed in the same category as a person who attended grades 10 − 12 only). This variable consisted of five levels: none, 1 − 3 years, 4 − 6 years, 7 − 9 years, 10 − 12 years. The number of persons at each level in the sample is shown in Table 1.2.

It would have been much better had the respondents been

TABLE 1.2

Frequency Distribution of the Sample by
Length of Attendance **in Parochial School**

Patterns of Attendance	Number of Years	Number of Laymen	Number of Clergy	Total Sample
None	None	949	29	976
A, G, J, or L	1 − 3	323	17	340
B, C, H, or K	4 − 6	68	11	79
D, E, or I	7 − 9	119	14	133
F	10 − 12	23	22	45
	Total	1,480	93	1,573

given opportunity to indicate exactly how many years and which grades they attended instead of their being limited to intervals of three grades each where checking the category might mean all three grades, or any two, or any one of the three. Therefore, the levels of length of attendance are not: none, 3 years, 6 years, 9 years, 12 years; but rather: none, from $1-3$ years, from $4-6$ years, from $7-9$ years, from $10-12$ years. The "length of attendance" variable was used to investigate the question, "Does more parochial school attendance produce, or at least correlate closely with, greater differences in beliefs, values, attitudes, opinions, and reported behaviors?"

Which grades attended. The second attendance variable was formed using only patterns A, G, J, and L from Table 1.1. It also consisted of five levels: no attendance, some or all of grades $1-3$ only, some or all of grades $4-6$ only, some or all of grades $7-9$ only, and some or all of grades $10-12$ only. The "grades attended" variable allowed investigation of the question, "If attendance is limited to three grades or less, does attending a specific set of three grades result in greater benefits?" Only a portion of the sample falls into the levels of this variable. See Table 1.3 for the numbers of persons involved.

TABLE 1.3

Grades Attended: **Frequency Distribution of Sample Cases Where Only Three Grades or Less Were Attended**

Patterns of Attendance	Grades Attended If Only 3 or Less	Number of Laymen	Number of Clergy	Sample Cases
None	None	947	29	976
A	Grades $1-3$ only	57	0	57
G	Grades $4-6$ only	56	2	58
J	Grades $7-9$ only	167	1	168
L	Grades $10-12$ only	43	14	57
	Total	1,270	46	1,316

Common attendance patterns. To avoid the artificiality of logical combinations that may not reflect empirical data, the third attendance variable was created roughly around the most common attendance patterns. It includes five levels as follows: 1 = no attendance; 2 = up to 6 years of attendance and approxi-

27

mately the first six grades; 3 = attending 6 – 9 years and approximately the first nine grades; 4 = attending some portion of grades 7 – 9 only; 5 = graduation from grade 12 no matter how many years of attendance preceding graduation. Use of this "common attendance patterns" variable allowed investigation of the question, "Are specific common patterns of attendance significantly better or worse? That is, are specific common patterns correlated with specific patterns of beliefs, values, attitudes, opinions, and reported behaviors? See Table 1.4 for the numbers in the sample in each level of the "common attendance patterns" variable.

TABLE 1.4

Frequency Distribution of the Sample by
Common Patterns of Attendance

Original Patterns of Attendance	Common Patterns of Attendance	Number of Laymen	Number of Clergy	Total Sample
None	None	947	29	976
A, B, or G	Through 6 yrs and 6th grade	139	3	142
C, D, or H	6 – 9 yrs and 9th grade	148	7	155
J	Some or all grades 7 – 9 only	167	1	168
E, F, I, K, or L	Through 12th grade	79	53	132
	Total	1,480	93	1,573

Combining the analyses of all three attendance variables amounts to investigating the question, "What characterizes attendance that maximizes the impact of parochial education?" This, at least, is the question that we would *like to be able* to answer. However, two qualifications must be made at this point.

First, this is a correlation study based on cross-sectional data. At best we will be able to report isolation of correlations that indicate some relationship between attending parochial school and holding certain beliefs and values, manifesting various attitudes and opinions, and reporting behaviors that are somewhat different from those of persons who never attended parochial school. In fact, by our data we are limited to a kind of process of elimination as we go about drawing our conclusions. We shall first *describe* parochial school attendees by contrast with those who have had no experience in parochial schools.

But to find significant differences between the two is by no means evidence for concluding that the parochial school attendees are different *because* they attended parochial school. We must rather seek alternative explanations by asking if we have evidence of any other variables that are highly correlated with parochial school attendance which might be the source of the differences. Only when we have controlled simultaneously for the possible effects of variables correlated with parochial school attendance and *find that the differences still persist* are we in a defensible position to make this tentative claim: on the basis of the evidence available it appears that attending parochial school has specific effects upon such-and-such people that seem to persist over so many years in certain ways. If we are able to eliminate one alternative explanation after another, we can gradually raise the probability of being right in concluding that these differences are the effects of parochial education. But even after eliminating all alternatives that our data allow us to investigate, we cannot be absolutely certain. We can only claim that there is a very high probability of our conclusions being correct in the long run. This state of affairs, of course, is not unique to this research. It is in the nature of scientific knowledge never to be absolute. Scientific knowledge at best is highly probable and tentative—true only until further notice.

The second qualification is partly a clarification. We had information only about length of attendance at some parochial school in some place at some time in history. We had no information about quality of participation. We had no information whatsoever about what specific schools were attended or where. Using a common social science research procedure, we controlled for the effects of such variables as quality of participation and the distinctive character of parishes, schools, and communities. We assumed these variables to be randomly distributed across the various individuals who gave us information about themselves. These individuals also were selected at random for participation in the *Study of Generations* from which our data were taken.

Readers who have additional questions about the quality of those data and the ways and precision with which they were collected should refer to the book, *A Study of Generations*, especially Chapter One, the introduction to Part Two, and Appendices A, B, and C, where very detailed information is provided. A copy of that book was given by Lutheran Brotherhood in the summer of 1972 to the library of every institution and parish in The Lutheran Church—Missouri Synod, Lutheran Church in America, and American Lutheran Church, with the expressed intent that it be made available to as wide a reading audience of pastors, teachers, and other parishioners as possible. Any member of these churches should be able to secure a copy on loan from his parish library or his pastor.

General Research Design

In summary, this research is a correlation study addressing the question: "Do Lutheran Church—Missouri Synod members ages 15—65 reporting differing amounts or types of parochial school attendance show systematically different patterns of belief, value, attitude, opinion, and reported behavior than LCMS members in general, and particularly those with no parochial school experience?" The three parochial school attendance variables described above (length of attendance, grades attended, pattern of attendance) are the independent variables (loosely speaking, the hypothetical "causes"). The 78 scales from *A Study of Generations* (consisting of 553 individual items) plus an additional 187 single items are the dependent variables (loosely speaking, the hypothetical "effects"). When investigating alternative explanations for significant differences found between persons reporting no parochial school attendance and some, the following additional characteristics were analyzed as independent variables in various combinations simultaneously with parochial school attendance and with each other: age, level of education ultimately attained (measured by a family level of education variable described later), and whether clergy or lay person (whether or not a person in later years received the addi-

30

tional parochial education involved in becoming a clergyman).

Exact age of all subjects in the study was known and allowed examination of one more generic question: "Are parochial schools having different impact now than they once did? That is, do persons who attended at different times in the last 60 years show different beliefs, values, attitudes, and behaviors?" The very precise technique of analysis of variance (ANOVA) was used to sort out the specific possible effects of (1) age alone; (2) parochial school attendance alone; and (3) the possible interaction of both age and parochial school attendance. Such an interaction would be interpreted as evidence that attendance at parochial school at different times in history had different effects.[3]

No attempt was made to identify subcategories within the portion of the sample that reported no parochial school attendance. Persons who had all kinds of parish education experiences other than day school attendance (from no parish education whatsoever through lifelong Sunday school attendance plus many years of church school teaching) were lumped together in the one category, "none" that is, no parochial school attendance. This means that the effects being sought were the effects of parochial school attendance that are different from, or in addition to, the effects of all other kinds of possible parish education experiences that had occurred in a representative sample of LCMS members ages 15 – 65. Therefore any differences or effects that are reported here as apparently the result of parochial school attendance are not the effects that might also be expected from attendance at Sunday school or adult instruction classes, or from all other parish education endeavors in which members had opportunity to participate.

Use of statistical tests and probability theory. As a result of this study we wanted to be able to say something not only about the sample of 1,573 people from the LCMS. We also wanted to draw conclusions about all members of the LCMS who had received all or part of the first 12 years of their education in parochial schools. Since we wanted to generalize to the whole church body, it was very important that the sample available from *A Study of Generations* was a representative probability sample (actually one person in every 667 was selected for study). Nevertheless, we could not assume that just because we found certain differences among subgroups in the sample those same differences would be found among the corresponding subgroups in the entire population of the LCMS. We were faced with the question, "When is a sample difference big enough to be taken as evidence that there likely is a comparable difference in the whole population?" Or, putting it another way, "Which differences between subgroups of the sample occur *because of differences in the subgroups of the population* from which the sample was drawn, and which sample differences occur *purely by chance* and thus are characteristic only of the sample?" Two standard statistical tests using the theorems of probability theory were employed to identify significant differences between the parochially educated and those not.

When scale scores were available, two- and three-way ar alyses of variance were used resulting in F-tests. When data w ere available only from single items, the chi-square was calculated. Throughout this report differences are reported as significant (i. e., true not only of the sample but also extremely likely to be true of the entire LCMS) only when statistical tests meet rigid criteria that were established before the results were known. The criteria were that the test results be such that there is less than one chance in 100 (and most of the time less than one chance in 1,000) that these results could have occurred purely by chance. Probability levels as stringent as these (.01 and .001) were selected for several reasons: the number of hypotheses to test, the size of the sample, and what was judged to constitute a *practical* difference.[4]

Limits of the study. The findings from this study can be used to draw conclusions only about LCMS members who were (1) in the summer of 1970 between the ages of 15 and 65 years, and (2) had attended an LCMS parochial elementary and secondary school sometime during the past 60 years. Classification as a parochial school attendee was limited to grades 1 – 12. Some of every classification including "none" may have attended church colleges. The grouping of attendance by intervals of three grades each is a definite limitation of the entire study. This is especially true of the grades 7 – 9 interval, which is not a natural grade grouping in most LCMS day schools. If a person indicated he attended in grades 7 – 9, he could mean he attended any one, or any two, or all three of those grades. It seems reasonable to believe that many additional important conclusions could have been reached had the data been collected expressly for this study so that attendance could have been broken down by grades. This is one of the tradeoffs for having a large body of unbiased data available for immediate analysis without cost of collection.

This research concerns parochial school *attendance* – nothing more. There is nothing that tells whether that attendance was by choice with eagerness, or by compulsion under duress. Nothing is known about the quality of participation while attending. Precisely when or where anyone in the sample attended a parochial school is not known. The research is limited to the possible effects of attending one or more of the first 12 grades of LCMS parochial schools – with the possible exception that someone in the sample who is now a member of LCMS attended parochial schools of another church body.

Finally, this study is limited to what can be learned from cross-sectional data – a snapshot, not a motion picture. This is not a longitudinal study of people over many years during which changes could be observed and possibly related to the previous experiences of the same people. All of the people who in this study reported attending Lutheran day schools could have experienced something else *in common* that caused all of them to be different from persons who did not attend parochial schools. *This study is limited to the claim that, within the boundaries of the available data, after all alternative explanatory variables have been controlled, parochial school attendance is the most*

33

likely explanation ("cause," if you please) *for the remaining differences in the profile of parochial school attendees when compared with the profile of those who attended other schools during grades 1 – 12.*

Synopsis of the report. Chapter Two will present a descriptive profile of LCMS members with parochial school experience by contrast with those never attending. The descriptive profile will be in terms of the dimensions and factors of *A Study of Generations.* No attempt at explanation will be offered either in terms of parochial school attendance or any other variable. The focus will merely be descriptive, on how those who at some time attended parochial elementary or high schools compare with those who never did.

Chapter Three will present analytic results addressed to the question, "Did they possibly get that way because they attended parochial schools?" The analysis will be an attempt to explain the differences in the profile of those who attended parochial schools on the basis of variables *other than* their parochial school attendance.

Chapter Four is a summary of conclusions and implications organized around the 13 questions raised in the beginning.

CHAPTER TWO

All Who Attended Parochial School — A Descriptive Profile

The ways in which the parochially educated were found to differ significantly on the average from persons who reported no parochial school attendance will be presented in terms of the dimensions and factors of *A Study of Generations*. Therefore, readers who are not already familiar with it may at this time want to read at least key portions of that book before going further.

In brief, 78 characteristics or properties of people (beliefs, values, attitudes, opinions, and behavior patterns) were identified in *A Study of Generations*. Each of these was assessed by one of 78 scales (64 parent scales and 14 subscales) made up of an average of approximately 10 items each that were first organized by factor and cluster analyses and then scaled by reciprocal averaging. This process of identification of characteristics and development of measuring scales is described briefly in Chapter 3 and the Introduction to Section II of *A Study of Generations*. It is described in greater detail on pages 335 through 348 of Appendix A of Section IV. The dimensions, or characteristics assumed to underlie the 64 parent scales, are described and named in Appendix B of Section IV. The specific questionnaire items that comprise the most important 56 of the parent scales are listed in Appendix C, also of Section IV of the same book.

The 64 parent scales were found to organize empirically into 14 major themes or factors. The process by which these factors or major groupings of characteristics were formed is described in brief in the Introduction to Section II of *A Study of Genera-*

tions and in greater detail on pages 348 and 349 of Appendix A, Section IV. The meaning of 12 of the 14 major themes (second-order factors) is discussed in depth in Chapters 4–9 of the same book.

Two Salient Findings

Before proceeding with a detailed descriptive profile of the ways in which the parochially educated do differ systematically and significantly from other Lutheran Church–Missouri Synod members, it is important to note two characteristic findings that showed up across one measure after another. First of all, there was no evidence to suggest that at any particular period of time has parochial schooling as a whole been significantly different throughout the last 60 years. To investigate this possibility three series of analyses of variance were performed. In each case two variables, the age of the respondent and his parochial school attendance, were investigated as they simultaneously related to the 78 measures of belief, value, attitude, and reported behavior.[1] In using the analysis of variance one might expect that if parochial schools in general had been significantly different sometime during the past 60 years, one would find many interactions between the two independent variables, age and parochial school attendance. (See Note 3, Chapter 1 for the reasoning behind this assumption.) This, however, did *not* prove to be the case. In the three series of analyses across the 78 scales, a total of 234 analyses of variance examining age and parochial school attendance, only 12 significant interactions were found: one in the first series where length of attendance was examined, five in the second series where grades attended were examined, and six in the third series where common patterns of attendance were examined.[2] This is surely not sufficient evidence for concluding that parochial schooling, at least as measured by these 78 scales, has generally been different at any time in the past 60 years than it showed itself to be in 1970.

This finding does *not*, however, reflect use of the new Mission:Life curriculum of The Lutheran Church–Missouri Synod and the new religion section of the 3-volume *Curriculum Guide for Lutheran Elementary Schools* written to correlate with that parish education curriculum. Neither was available until 1971 after these data were collected. Furthermore, it does not seem reasonable to expect that persons included in this study would have been able to experience much, if any, of the change in the teaching of religion that has been taking place during the last 10 years. In the early 1960s some professors of theology and religious education on the synodical teachers college campuses attempted to give added attention to the affective realm and the resulting implications for content and methodology. But their students would not have been teaching in parochial schools long enough to expect those emphases to have influenced the results of this study. Future research in parochial education, however, should look for specific effects of this break from the more restrictive cognitive approach to the teaching of religion.

A second consistent finding in this research suggests that the differences between those who report some parochial school attendance and those who do not may actually be due to parochial school attendance and not some other influence. The finding is this: There is a general tendency for differences in beliefs, values, attitudes, and opinions to be greater as more years of parochial school attendance are reported. Where differences occur between those who report no attendance and some attendance, there is generally a high correlation between the size of that difference and the number of years attended. Table 2.1 illustrates this most clearly for the entire sample.

Scores on the scales in Table 2.1 for groups reporting varying amounts of parochial school attendance do not show the widest ranges of difference that were found. However, they do, in each case, show a clear progression from lowest scores for those reporting none up through highest scores for those reporting 10−12 years of attendance.

Slight variations from such an orderly sequence of average subgroup scores could be expected from a sample even though corresponding subgroups of the population might still have scores on the average that progressively increase with increased

TABLE 2.1

Scales Most Clearly Showing Strong Positive Correlation Between Standardized* Scores and Length of Parochial School Attendance (Mean = 50.0; Standard Deviation = 10.0)

Scale No.	Scale Name	Length of Parochial School Attendance					
		None	1 – 3 yrs	4 – 6 yrs	7 – 9 yrs	10 – 12 yrs	Probability
8	Biblical Knowledge	49.9	50.2	54.1	54.9	61.1	< .0001
14	A Personal, Caring God	49.9	50.1	52.1	52.1	53.9	< .01
16	The Exclusive Truth Claim of Christianity (Exaggerated)	49.0	52.3	52.2	52.1	55.0	< .0001
21	Personal Evangelism	49.9	53.0	54.3	54.4	65.2	< .0001
41	Practices of Personal Piety	49.7	51.8	53.3	53.8	63.4	< .00001
60	Individual Christian Responsibility	50.2	50.0	52.0	52.2	55.6	< .0001
61	Image of Lutherans as Different	49.7	50.2	50.7	52.2	54.2	< .01
70	Gospel-Oriented Life	49.9	50.6	51.8	52.7	56.5	< .0001
74	Personal Initiative on Church and Public Issues	51.1	51.9	54.7	54.6	68.6	< .0001
	Number in the sample:	968	334	78	129	44	

* Average scale scores per group have been standardized on the basis of the mean and standard deviation for Lutheran Church – Missouri Synod *lay people* for each scale. However, since groups include both clergy and lay people, weighted scores for rows are not necessarily 50.0.

numbers of years of parochial school attendance. Scales with variations in average scores that are still positively correlated with number of years attended are shown in Table 2.2.

Though scores in Table 2.2 definitely show the same pattern of positive correlation between amount of the characteristic measured and the number of years of attending parochial schools, scores for two groups most commonly show variation from perfect order: 1 – 3 years and 7 – 9 years. Scale 51 shows the most extreme variation on the part of the 1 – 3 year group, and Scales 40 and 42 show the most extreme variations for the 7 – 9 year group. The only notable exception to these two patterns of variation is in Scale 44 where it is the 4 – 6 year group that breaks order.

The same tendency for either the 1 – 3 year group or the 7 – 9 year group, or both, to vary slightly from the ordered sequence manifests itself again among scales where average scores tend

38

TABLE 2.2

Additional Scales for Which Average Standardized Scores Are Not Perfectly Ordered but Are Still Positively Correlated with Length of Parochial School Attendance (Average for Lutheran Church—Missouri Synod Lay People = 50.0; Standard Deviation = 10.0)

Scale No.	Scale Name	None	1–3 yrs	4–6 yrs	7–9 yrs	10–12 yrs	Probability
5	Humanity of Jesus	50.8	49.6	53.0	51.5	61.4	< .0001
6	Divinity of Jesus	48.9	51.1	54.3	53.7	57.2	< .0001
12	The Church, Me, and Social Justice	50.0	50.3	52.7	52.1	56.1	< .001
19	Religious Experience	48.9	52.7	51.8	51.9	54.5	< .0001
28	Transcendental Meaning in Life	49.5	50.5	52.9	52.3	54.8	< .0001
40	Congregational Activity	49.8	51.5	53.5	52.3	60.8	< .00001
42	The Role of Pastors in Social Issues	49.9	50.2	53.0	50.7	55.4	< .01
44	Fundamentalism-Liberalism	49.4	51.0	50.4	51.7	52.8	< .01
47	Personal Involvement in Church and Community	50.6	49.9	52.7	53.3	61.3	< .0001
48	Personal Involvement in Church	50.5	50.1	52.5	53.4	60.7	< .0001
51	Acceptance of Authority	50.8	48.0	52.0	51.7	52.6	< .0001
55	Family Education	51.2	48.8	53.0	52.3	59.7	< .0001
58	Awareness of the Immanent Trinity	50.0	49.8	54.0	53.7	55.3	< .0001
66	Emotional Certainty of Faith	50.0	50.0	51.7	51.4	54.1	< .01
71	Attitudes Toward Life and Death	50.0	49.5	52.3	52.2	53.8	< .001

to correlate *negatively* with number of years of parochial school attended, as shown in Table 2.3.

Tables 2.1, 2.2, and 2.3 all clearly show that there is a definite tendency for whatever is associated with parochial school attendance to be correlated in such a way that the longer the parochial school attendance the greater the characteristic difference from those who report no attendance (with the exception of Scales 36, 52, 57, and 63 in Table 2.3). Nevertheless, the patterns of slight, and sometimes not so slight, variation from ordered sequence (though they may be just random fluctuations) provide a clue suggesting that there may be something system-

TABLE 2.3

**Scales for Lay People and Clergy Showing Negative Correlation
Between Average Standardized Scores and Length of Parochial
School Attendance (Average for Lutheran Church — Missouri Synod
lay people = 50.0; Standard Deviation = 10.0)**

Scale No.	Scale Name	None	1 – 3 yrs	4 – 6 yrs	7 – 9 yrs	10 – 12 yrs	Probability
9	Biblical Ignorance	50.0	50.0	47.0	47.1	42.1	< .0001
10	Prior Denominational Membership (Large Den.)	51.9	48.5	46.0	46.4	44.7	< .00001
15	Salvation by Works	49.7	50.6	45.3	45.8	35.9	< .0001
27	Disappointment with the Church	49.6	51.0	49.6	48.9	43.7	< .0001
29	Values of Self-Development	49.5	50.7	48.5	48.5	45.9	< .01
32	Prejudice Against the Poor and the Disadvantaged	49.8	50.5	44.6	47.4	42.0	< .0001
34	Generalized Prejudice	49.6	50.7	45.2	46.9	43.9	< .0001
36	Christian Utopianism	49.1	51.8	49.8	50.6	50.0	< .01
37	Need for Unchanging Structure	49.2	51.8	45.9	48.9	45.2	< .0001
38	Need for Unchanging Family Structure	48.6	50.9	46.7	48.7	45.9	< .001
43	Need for Religious Absolutism	49.5	51.0	47.9	48.9	43.9	< .001
52	Need for a Dependable World	49.2	51.9	49.4	48.3	49.0	< .001
54	Desire for Detachment from the World	49.2	51.6	47.8	49.8	45.5	< .001
56	Social Distance — Radical Life Styles	49.4	50.6	45.6	47.5	44.4	< .001
57	Social Distance — Race and Religion	49.0	51.7	48.0	48.7	48.4	< .01
62	Service Without Proclamation	49.6	50.2	48.1	48.2	44.6	< .01
63	Peer Orientation	49.1	51.6	52.0	50.2	48.6	< .001
64	Power Orientation to Social Issues	49.6	51.1	48.9	47.8	43.5	< .0001
67	Self-Oriented Utilitarianism	49.3	51.2	48.8	47.9	41.0	< .0001
69	Horatio Alger Orientation	49.4	51.8	48.4	49.9	46.4	< .01

atically different about the effect (indeed, if these are *effects* of attending parochial school) of (a) attending no more than three grades of parochial school, or (b) attending some parts of grades 7 – 9. This is suggested by the fact that the 1 – 3 year group is made up entirely of persons who attended only 3 years of parochial school or less. Second, nearly half of those in the $1-3$ group attended only some or all of grades $7-9$. Third, what is unique to those who attended $7-9$ *years* is, of course, that for the most part they attended *grades* $7-9$. The matter of the possible distinctive influences of such parochial school attendance patterns will be investigated more thoroughly in Chapter 3.

For all of the scales reported in Tables 2.1 through 2.3, average scores for the five groups by length of attendance were such that, in all except two cases, the group reporting no attendance scored significantly differently from at least one of the groups reporting some parochial school attendance. The two exceptions were scales 29 and 69, Values of Self-Development and Horatio Alger Orientation, where the $1-3$ year group alone was significantly different from the $10-12$ year group alone.

The probabilities listed in the last column of Tables 2.1 through 2.3 indicate the chances of getting sample subgroup average scores as different as these purely by chance if, in fact, the corresponding subgroups of the entire population of all members of The Lutheran Church—Missouri Synod from whom these respondents were randomly sampled, were *not* different. For example, a probability of less than ($<$) .00001 indicates that there is less than one chance in 100,000 that attendance-group differences as large as these could have occurred in our sample purely by chance and for no other cause.

A Descriptive Profile of the Parochially Educated

From a careful comparison of the titles of the scales in Tables 2.1 and 2.2 by contrast with those in Table 2.3, one can readily see not only that persons who attended parochial schools scored significantly differently on various measures of beliefs, values, and attitudes. They also scored higher on scales that assess what might be generally agreed to be more positive characteristics. And the parochially educated scored lower on scales that generally measure less desirable characteristics.

However, so far, scales have been presented *only* for which *significant differences* in scores were found between attending and not-attending groups. Measures for which no significant differences for such groups were found also provide an equally interesting set of findings. Furthermore, grouping the various scales by the major themes or factors into which they organized themselves in *A Study of Generations* provides a clearer, more diversified, and much more comprehensive picture.

The 14 *A Study of Generations* factors organize logically under four topics: (1) beliefs and values, (2) law orientation, (3) mission and ministry of the church, and (4) personal involvement and service. The overall profile of the parochially educated will be presented factor by factor under these four topics in terms of the degree to which those who attended parochial schools tend to differ from those who did not. In Tables 2.4 through 2.16 that follow, plus and minus signs will be used to indicate whether the scores of the parochially educated were on the average significantly higher or lower, as follows:

+ + + = *much higher* for parochially educated (usually a half standard deviation or more, 5 standardized score points or more, between those not attending at all and those attending 9 – 12 years; less than one chance in 100,000 of such differences occurring purely by chance)

+ + = *higher* (those attending 9 – 12 years scoring on the average .3 to .4 of a standard deviation higher than those not attending; less than one chance in 1,000 of such a difference occurring by chance alone)

+ = *slightly higher* (about one-fourth of a standard deviation higher for those attending up to 12 years; less than one chance in 100 of such a difference occurring by chance alone)

Blank = *no significant difference*

— = *slightly lower* (about a one-fourth standard deviation lower scores on the average for those attending up to 12 years; probability of such a difference by chance alone less than .01)

− −   = *lower* (.3 to .4 of a standard deviation lower on the average for those attending up to 12 years; probability of such difference by chance alone less than .001 or less than .0001)

− − −   = *much lower* for parochially educated (one-half standard deviation or more difference; probability less than .00001)

+ +− −   = *higher* with a few years, but *lower* with more years of parochial school

+ −   = *slightly higher* with a few years, but *slightly lower* with more years of parochial school

− +   = *slightly lower* with a few years, but *slightly higher* with more years of parochial school

− −+ + = *lower* with a few years, but *higher* with more years of parochial school

Each of the scales listed in a single table clusters around one theme. All of the scales in a single table, to a greater or lesser degree, have something in common. Because this is the case, each table contains one column entitled, "Load." "Load" is shorthand for factor loading. A Factor loading is a kind of correlation, a measure of the degree to which a single scale, in this case, is related to that which all of the scales in a given table share in common. It is a measure of the degree to which the scale is related to the theme or factor that that set of scales share in common.

Factor loadings can be as high as 1.0 and as low as 0. They can be positive or negative, so their range runs from + 1.0 to − 1.0. Notice that in each table the scales are arranged in order such that the factor loadings run in sequence from the highest positive loading to the lowest positive loading through 0 to the lowest negative loading up through the highest negative loading. This indicates that another way of looking at the theme or factor that this set of scales share in common is as a dimension or a continuum. If a given scale would have a factor loading of

+1.0, that would mean that that scale would be measuring exactly the same thing as whatever it is that the whole set of scales has to a lesser or greater degree in common. That scale and the factor or theme would be identical. If a scale were to have a factor loading of −1.0, that would mean that that scale is assessing in a sense just the opposite of what the set of scales share to a greater or lesser degree in common. The scale would be just the opposite of the factor or theme.

Therefore, to get a sense of what the factor or theme is all about, one needs to study the scales that cluster about the theme or that make up the factor. When doing so, give the scales with the highest factor loadings, whether positive or negative, the heaviest weight or the greater consideration as you try to get a fuller grasp of what the theme or factor really is. If, as in the case of Table 2.4, there is quite an array of both positively and negatively related scales, it may be helpful to think of the theme running through all of these scales as a dimension, one pole of which is identified by the scales with the highest positive loadings and the other pole of which is identified by the scales with the highest negative loadings.

This whole process, of course, emphasizes the importance of understanding and being familiar with each of the scales. Their titles have been chosen to be maximally descriptive; nevertheless, this is one more reason for becoming as familiar as possible with each of the scales by pursuing it through *A Study of Generations* by making ample use of Appendices B and C and the Index of that book.

Before considering each factor in detail, it is important to remember that many of the characteristics and activities in which the parochially educated excel are also more typical of pastors than lay people. These differences may or may not be due to the disproportionate large number of clergy in the parochial school sample when compared to the ratio of pastors to lay people in the entire Lutheran Church—Missouri Synod. Chapter 3 will deal fully with that issue. What follows next is a detailed profile of the parochially educated, both lay people and clergy.

Beliefs and Values

The system of beliefs that was by far the most pervasive and consistent among all of those identified in *A Study of Generations* is called The Heart of Lutheran Piety. In fact, this factor represents more of a way of life than merely a set of beliefs. It consists of scales that assess beliefs, values, attitudes, and sets or syndromes of behavior. In fact, if there is any one factor that Christian educators would probably unanimously agree represents a set of characteristics or way of life that they would like Christians to possess or exemplify, The Heart of Lutheran Piety is the factor. It was used in *A Study of Generations* to assess Gospel orientation as opposed to orientation to the Law, structure, conformity, and rigidity. This is not to say that the 14 measures that together comprise this factor provide a fix on *everything* that might be called life in the Gospel. It does say that of all the sets of measures that formed empirically into families or major themes, this set comes the closest to characterizing life in the Gospel as opposed to natural religion or the unbelief of life under the Law apart from Christ.

If there is any aspect of life in the Gospel that is conspicuous by its absence from The Heart of Lutheran Piety, it is social conscience together with participation in the constant struggle for social justice and a society that is both humanitarian in its goals and the effects of its structures. This aspect of life in the Gospel, about which so much concern has been voiced during the past few years within and without the church, was distinct enough to be a separate theme in itself (Factor Three). The kind of Gospel orientation that is most distinctly The Heart of Lutheran Piety is summarized in Table 2.4.

The profile of persons who report attending parochial schools is very different for The Heart of Lutheran Piety from the profile of those who report no parochial school attendance. Viewing The Heart of Lutheran Piety as a continuum with a positive and a negative pole, notice first that the parochially educated on the average tend to score higher on those measures that comprise the positive end of the continuum and on the average tend

45

TABLE 2.4

The Heart of Lutheran Piety (Factor One)

Parochial School Differences	Load	Scale	Dimension Title
Positive			
+ +	.80	28	Transcendental Meaning in Life
+	.74	14	A Personal, Caring God
+	.73	66	Emotional Certainty of Faith
+	.72	44	Fundamentalism – Liberalism
	.67	46	Importance of Christian Practices in My Life
+ +	.65	71	Attitude Toward Life and Death
+ + +	.55	41	Personal Piety
+ +	.54	19	Religious Experience
+ +	.52	58	Awareness of the Immanent Trinity
+ +	.52	6	Divinity of Jesus
+ +	.48	16	The Exclusive Truth Claim of Christianity Exaggerated
+ –	.44	36	Christian Utopianism
Negative			
– –	−.29	15	Salvation by Works
+ –	−.32	29	Values of Self-Development

to score lower on those scales that comprise the negative pole of the continuum.

Table 2.4 indicates that those who attended parochial schools were much more heavily involved in practices of personal piety such as cooperating with their pastors, giving money to the church, reading the Bible and literature about the faith, talking about Christianity and the church, spending time in meditation, and generally trying to put their faith into practice. On the average they placed higher value on the transcendental dimension of life and showed more positive attitudes toward life and people, including a view of death as a friend rather than an enemy or the unknown. They also reported a significantly higher incidence of personal religious experience, awareness of the triune God's presence in their own lives, belief in Jesus' divinity, and acceptance of the exclusive truth claim of Christianity that salvation is to be found in Jesus Christ alone. They also tended more characteristically to describe their God as a personal God who cares for them in their own daily lives through Jesus Christ.

to exhibit emotional assurance of their faith, to assent to conservative doctrine, and to hold to Christian utopianism of the sort that includes the belief that all of the world's problems would be solved if each individual became a Christian. They were significantly less inclined to believe that they are saved by doing good works; and, quite interestingly, those who reported attending parochial schools for just a few years tended to place a somewhat higher value on individual and personal development while those who reported attending more years, and particularly as many as 12 years, tended to place slightly less value on personal development as compared with those who attended no parochial schools.

More specifically, notice that at the two opposite ends of this factor are measures of what people value (Scales 28 and 29). The results concerning Scales 28 and 29 show that those who attended parochial schools, by scoring significantly higher on the average on Transcendental Meaning in Life, therefore definitely tend more commonly to believe in miracles, life after death, and the existence of the devil. At the same time they value love, salvation, family happiness, forgiveness, religion, ethical living, and service to other people. By contrast they are significantly less inclined to place high value on adventure or exploration, being personally important or well liked, pleasure and fun, independence, making their own choices, making a lot of money, having influence or authority over others, physical appearance, beauty, possessing skills, or achieving their own personal goals.

There is some danger of misinterpreting the results concerning Scales 14, 66, 44, and 46. The fact that persons who attended parochial schools scored only slightly higher on the first three of those scales and on the average about the same as persons reporting no attendance in the case of Scale 46, Importance of Christian Practices in My Life, may be as much due to the characteristics of these scales as to the characteristics of the parochially educated. Lutherans on the average tend to score very high on all four of these measures. For Lutherans these four scales have a low ceiling. For example, in terms of raw scale scores, the potential range for Scale 46, Importance of Christian Practices in My Life, is from a low of 7 to a high of 36. The average score for Lutheran clergy is 35.9 and for Lutheran lay people 35.5. That doesn't leave much room for improvement on the part of those attending parochial school or of any other group! This situation is somewhat less extreme but nevertheless still the case for Scale 14 concerning belief in a personal, caring God, and for Scale 66, Emotional Certainty of Faith.

The danger of misinterpretation is even greater in the case of Scale 44, Fundamentalism—Liberalism, and Scale 16, The Exclusive Truth Claim of Christianity Exaggerated, unless one is very familiar with the characteristics and meanings of these scales. Very high scores in either case might carry some negative implications depending upon one's theological stance. Very high scores on Scale 44 would indicate an exaggerated exclusivism and commitment to fundamentalistic dogma. It would mean being ready to say:

"I strongly agree. Persons who disbelieve this are not true to the Christian faith," to statements such as the following: "The Bible is the Word of God. God inspired men to report verbally what he said. The Bible in the original text contains no errors." "Today, just as at Pentecost, the gift of the Holy Spirit is evidenced by the person speaking in unknown tongues. This promise should be claimed in modern churches." "The belief that human beings descended from some lower animal form is contrary to the Word of God and unChristian." "The nature of man is that he is absolutely and completely evil, totally depraved, and there is nothing good in him."

The possible range of raw scores on Scale 44 is from 35 to 115. The average score for all Lutheran clergy was 95.1 and for all Lutheran lay people was 93.3. These average scores were interpreted in *A Study of Generations* as indicating that the weight of Lutheranism is on a conservative belief system. It is neither fundamentalistic nor liberal in terms of doctrinal statements such as those quoted above and other traditional Christian belief statements concerning the Virgin Birth, the Resurrection, the Second Coming, the Atonement, miracles, Baptism, Holy Communion, the Ten Commandments, and the Power of the Keys. These average scores also indicate a tendency to agree with the initial statement, but not to require that another person agree exactly in order to be a true Christian. The average score for laymen in The Lutheran Church—Missouri Synod alone is 97.3, which is significantly higher than the average for all Lutheran laymen but far from being fundamentalistic on the average. But it is clear that more lay members of The Lutheran Church—Missouri Synod tend toward a stronger conservative stance than do laymen of the ALC and LCA.

In the light of this, how then do LCMS members who attended parochial schools score on the average? In terms of raw scale scores, the five groups of LCMS members by length of parochial school attendance score on the average as follows:

None	= 96.8	4 – 6 years	= 97.7
1 – 3 years	= 90.2	7 – 9 years	= 98.8
	9 – 12 years	= 98.8	

Though significantly higher statistically (p = .01), this difference of approximately one-third of a standard deviation between persons with no parochial school attendance and those attending up to 12 years is still not large enough to indicate other than a slightly more conservative stance, but surely not a fundamentalistic one on the part of those educated in parochial schools.

Extremely high scores on Scale 16, The Exclusive Truth Claim of Christianity Exaggerated, indicate the exaggerated belief that the "true church" is clearly known and, thus, its enemies are clearly known. This distortion of the exclusive claims of Lutheran theology often expresses itself in the claim that there is salvation to be found only in a single denomination or even a particular branch of a denomination or a single congregation. Extremely low scores on Scale 16 indicate rejection of belief both in one "true church" and salvation only in Christ.

Scores about two-fifths of the way up on the range of possible scores for this scale indicate belief in one "true church" and salvation only through Jesus Christ—which is traditional Lutheran doctrine. Lutherans on the average score at about this latter point, that is, an average for lay people of 63.5 and for clergy of 65.5 out of a range of 45 through 94. Average raw scores for the five subgroups by length of parochial school attendance, beginning with those reporting none, were as follows: 65.5, 68.4, 68.3, 68.2, and 70.7. As can be seen from Table 2.1, this represents six-tenths of a standard deviation between those reporting no attendance and those attending through 12 years. This is a substantial increase but still not an exaggeration of the exclusive truth claims of Christianity and Lutheran theology. Rather, it indicates a significantly stronger tendency to affirm belief in one "true church" and salvation exclusively in Jesus Christ. In fact, in terms of scale scores, 70.7 stands exactly halfway between rejection of salvation by faith in Jesus Christ alone and the distorted claim that the only "true church" is a clearly identifiable congregation, organization, or denomination.

Some more specific indications of orientation to the Gospel are picked up by Factor Fourteen which is described in Table 2.5.

TABLE 2.5
More Specific Gospel-Orientation (Factor Fourteen)

Parochial School Differences	Load	Scale	Dimension Title
	Positive		
+ +	.44	70	Gospel-Oriented Life
+ +	.38	5	Humanity of Jesus
+ + +	.30	8	Biblical Knowledge
	Negative		
+ −	−.32	69	Horatio Alger Orientation

Two members of the Study of Generations research team, while developing the instrumentation for that study, attempted to create a single scale to measure orientation to the Gospel.

They were partially successful in this attempt. A scale did form from among the items that they developed, but only some of the intended items formed the scale. The overall reliability of that scale was only .50, one of the lowest in the entire study. Furthermore, it became clear while data were being analyzed that the respondents could have consistently selected the "Gospel" response for each of the items in Scale 70 for a reason other than being oriented to the Gospel.[3] Nevertheless, when one looks at the fact that in Factor Fourteen, Scale 69 — Horatio Alger Orientation — is the opposite pole from Scale 70 — Gospel-Oriented Life, one has further evidence that Scale 70 measures the opposite of an orientation to Law or the pulling up of one's self by one's bootstraps represented by Horatio Alger Orientation.

To interpret the significance of the fact that those who attended parochial schools tended to give more affirmation to the humanity of Jesus, it is important to remember that *A Study of Generations* found that Lutherans generally tend so to emphasize the divinity of Jesus as almost to deny his humanity. The most extreme difference between clergy and lay people found in *A Study of Generations* concerned beliefs about the humanity of Jesus. Clergy on the average scored a standard deviation and a half higher on belief in the humanity of Jesus than did lay people. Clergy generally tended to give evidence of seeing Jesus as both truly human and truly God, while lay people in general evidenced very strong tendencies to deny the true humanity of Jesus. The parochially educated, in this case, too, more closely resembled clergy than did the LCMS sample as a whole.

The measure of Biblical knowledge used in this study represents a very rudimentary level of Biblical knowledge. Therefore, the very significant difference in average scores between those with no parochial schooling and those with some or much may represent little more than the difference between practical Biblical ignorance and some basic knowledge of the Scriptures. However, since this is another case where the ceiling of the scale is really quite low when it comes to measuring any *substantial* knowledge of the Bible, it is possible that those who received education in parochial schools were more significantly Biblically literate than is indicated by the results of this research. Any future research specifically planned to assess the impact of parochial education should, of course, include more far-ranging measures of Biblical knowledge.

The most significant aspect of the findings concerning Biblical knowledge have to do with the fact that greater Biblical knowledge is associated with greater affirmation of the humanity of Jesus, with tendencies to live out the Gospel in relationship with other people, and with a rejection of works-righteousness. And there is no particular evidence here that the Biblical knowledge so characteristic of parochial school graduates is strongly associated with a need for religious absolutism or rigidity of personality.

Factor Seven concerns meaning and purpose in life as shown in Table 2.6. The positive end of this factor is characterized by a sense of purpose and meaning in one's own life and work. The negative end is characterized by anxiety over such aspects

TABLE 2.6

Meaning and Purpose in Life (Factor Seven)

Parochial School Differences	Load	Scale	Dimension Title
Positive			
	.70	68	Life Purpose
	.30	50	Acceptance of Middle-Class Norms
Negative			
	−.68	17	Feelings of Isolation and Pressure
	−.70	49	Anxiety over My Faith

of faith as whether or not one will go to heaven, not being able to give a good reason for one's faith, not being close enough to Christ, finding it difficult to believe the church's teachings or not living up to one's Christian convictions, finding it hard to share one's faith in a natural way, and desiring a deeper faith in God. There was no evidence that either of these aspects of the factor were more characteristic of those who attended parochial school than of those who did not.

Relationships with God and with other persons are most highly valued by most Lutherans. Of the three views of the "good life" presented in Table 2.7, by far the most popular among Lutherans as a whole are (1) desire for a stable, dependable world, and (2) desire for a controllable world. To be able to live in a world that I can depend on is more frequently valued by older people among Lutherans in general. To prefer detachment from the world and to seek to explore the inner self is more common among both the very young and the very old. To value being able to control the world I live in is more characteristic of the highly educated among Lutherans as a whole.

As will be reported later, there is a tendency for those who report the most parochial education also to report that they are older and that they have more years of formal education. Therefore, one might expect that the parochially educated would show greater tendencies to value a controllable world and a dependable world. Instead, those who went to parochial schools for just a few years expressed greater desires for detachment from the world and life in a dependable world than those who reported longer attendance — up to 12 years. The latter expressed about the same amount of desire for all of these types of the "good life" as did those reporting no parochial education. In other words, the only views of the "good life" characteristically different for the parochially educated showed up among those who reported from one to six years of parochial school attendance.

TABLE 2.7

Views of the Good Life (Factor Ten)

Parochial School Differences	Load	Scale	Dimension Title
	Positive		
	.75	53	Desire for a Controllable World
+ + − −	.65	54	Desire for Detachment from the World
+ + − −	.58	52	Desire for a Dependable World

53

This implies that a little parochial school attendance may be associated with inclinations toward a monastic life (Scale 54) of stability and security. (Scale 52)

Law and Gospel

One of the most important findings from *A Study of Generations* concerned the two theological constructs, Law and Gospel. It was found that Law and Gospel are not just two interesting ideas about which theologians have been thinking and writing for centuries. Nor are they irrelevant and outdated first or 16th century concepts that do not fit contemporary believers' frames of reference. Rather, they are two contrasting and dramatically different ways of life. Best described theologically as "orientation to the Gospel" and "orientation to life under the Law," these are the two most common perspectives of life held by Lutherans in 1970.

Of the two, life in the Gospel was much more difficult to describe and to assess. It is in the very nature of the Gospel to be free, creative, alive, dynamically changing, and difficult, if not impossible, to limit. Factor One or The Heart of Lutheran Piety as described above is a necessary but not a *sufficient* or full set of indicators of life in the Gospel.

The rigidity, compelling conformity, and the conviction that the reality of life is to be found in its order and structure so characteristic of life under the Law, is assessed by Factor Two called Misbelief or Life Under the Law. More scales (16) cluster around this major theme than around any other theme that is characteristic of some Lutherans.

Most Christian educators would expect natural man who has not been confronted by the Gospel or who has rejected the Gospel to exhibit the essential misbelief which is life under the Law. And Christian educators would consistently try to minimize this orientation to the never-ending demands and requirements of life under Law. Therefore, pastors, teachers, and fellow Christians alike would surely want those who attended parochial schools to show less of the characteristics of Law orientation than might

be found among church members who have never attended parochial schools. Table 2.8 shows this generally to be the case.

TABLE 2.8

Misbelief or Life Under the Law (Factor Two)

Parochial School Difference	Load	Scale	Dimension Title
	Positive		
+ + − −	.76	37	Need for Unchanging Structure
− −	.70	43	Need for Religious Absolutism
+ + − −	.69	34	Generalized Prejudice
− −	.69	56	Social Distance – Radical Life Styles
+ −	.65	57	Social Distance – Racial and Religious Groups
− −	.53	67	Self-Oriented Utilitarianism
+ +	.49	16	The Exclusive Truth Claim of Christianity Exaggerated
	.47	26	Mutual Support Among Church, Society, and Individuals
+ −	.44	36	Christian Utopianism
− −	.38	15	Salvation by Works
+ −	.36	69	Horatio Alger Orientation
	.32	35	Pessimism
	Negative		
+	−.34	42	The Role of Pastors in Social Action
	−.35	65	Church Involvement in Social Issues
+ +	−.36	5	Humanity of Jesus
+ +	−.42	55	Family Education Level

However, here again are some indications that a little parochial education may be worse than none at all, that is, if one
assumes that these characteristic differences are the effects of
attending or not attending parochial schools.

As indicated earlier in this chapter, those who attend parochial schools just a few years score higher on measures of certain
characteristics than those who attend more years. On these same
characteristics the latter score the same or considerably lower
than those who have not attended parochial schools. This effect
shows up even more among the various measures of misbelief
or life under the Law. It is particularly noticeable in Scale 37,
which measures a need for keeping family and society structures

55

exactly as they are—in a sense not rocking the boat, and Scale 34 which measures generally prejudicial attitudes. These attitudes include regular use of stereotypes and willingness to agree with a variety of statements that are derogatory to blacks, the poor, Indians, Jews, and other minority or disadvantaged peoples. This same tendency is indicated to a lesser degree in the following scales:

A. Scale 57 that measures a desire to keep socially distant from people who are racially and religiously different from one's self;

B. Scale 36 which measures the belief that all the world's problems can be solved if each individual were to become a Christian—a belief with almost a magical flavor; and

C. Scale 69, the Horatio Alger perspective that everyone can succeed if he will just work at it hard enough.

Apart from the tendency indicated in the preceding paragraph, those who reported the most parochial school attendance consistently differed significantly from those who did not attend by (1) scoring consistently lower on the various measures characterizing the positive end of the misbelief factor, and (2) by scoring consistently either slightly higher or definitely higher on three out of four of the scales that characterize the negative end. Those who reported the most parochial school attendance scored consistently lower on all except three of the misbelief measures and slightly or definitely higher on all except one of the measures that are most highly negatively correlated with misbelief or life under the Law.

Scale 16, The Exclusive Truth Claim of Christianity Exaggerated, seems to be the one exception to the pattern. But recalling our earlier discussion of Scale 16 concerning The Heart of Lutheran Piety, the increase in scores characteristic of the parochially educated is not the extreme and legalistic claim that salvation by grace through faith in Christ is to be found only in a certain identifiable group or organization. Therefore, these findings on Scale 16 are consistent with the rest of the profile of the parochially educated concerning misbelief.

The last scale in Table 2.8 is a measure combining a report of the respondent's educational level and his report of his spouse's and both his parents' level of education. Despite the fact that the average level of education of younger Lutherans is significantly higher than that of their predecessors, there is enough consistency of educational level within families for Scale 55 to have a reliability of .70. This measure shows that those who reported attending parochial schools for the longest period of time also eventually received more formal education on the average than persons who reported no parochial school attendance.

Table 2.8 also shows that the more highly educated are less inclined to manifest prejudicial attitudes, to view life primarily as demand, and to believe the essence of reality to be in the structures, organization, and order of things. This raises the question as to whether the parochially educated are less Law oriented because of their parochial education or simply because they received more formal education. Whatever the cause, those who reported attending parochial schools for a few years tended to be somewhat more Law oriented than those never attending, while those who attended parochial school 7 – 12 years tended to be considerably less Law oriented than those who never attended.

These characteristics are also consistent with the findings concerning Factor Eleven, Self-Orientation or Natural Religion. This factor is shown in Table 2.9 and is characterized by Biblical ignorance, questionable personal behavior, placing highest value on personal improvement and aggrandizement, and belief in salvation by works. It is the logical opposite of Factor Fourteen discussed above. Factor Fourteen showed that people who knew their Bibles tended most often to relate to other people in ways characterized by the Gospel. Factor Eleven in Table 2.9 shows Biblical ignorance to be significantly correlated with natural religion of works-righteousness, values that are highly self-centered, and behavior that is at least unwholesome and in many ways just plain sinful.

TABLE 2.9

Self-Orientation or Natural Religion (Factor Eleven)

Parochial School Difference	Load	Scale	Dimension Title
		Positive	
– –	.54	9	Biblical Ignorance
	.42	23	Questionable Personal Activities
+ –	.36	29	Values of Self-Development
– –	.33	15	Salvation by Works

Here too, the profile for those who attended parochial schools is consistent with what we have already seen. They are on the average less Biblically ignorant. That is, they are less mistaken about their knowledge of the facts or content of the Bible. On the average they are significantly less inclined to believe that they will be saved by attempting to please God with their good works. And those who attended parochial school at least 4 years or more are much less attracted by things such as power, prestige, adventure, money, personal achievement, skill, and physical beauty.

The data show that the parochially educated report no less participation in questionable and sinful activities such as swearing, fighting, committing adultery, and the like. This is the first indication reported thus far that parochial school attendance appears to be much more closely related to beliefs, values, and attitudes than it does to behavior. Here above all is a set of personal behaviors where one would expect some differences. But there are none. Rather, the parochially educated differ significantly not so much in what they do not do, but in what they do more of, or in what they do differently (see Scale 41 in Table 2.4 and Scale 70 in Table 2.5).

Two other ways in which those who attended parochial schools are not different are indicated by Scales 26 and 35 in Table 2.8. The parochially educated are apparently no more or less pessimistic. Nor are they more or less inclined to expect that other people and institutions in society should be supportive of a single way of life rather than a variety.

Scale 29 in Table 2.9 again adds to the growing indications that a little parochial school attendance may in some ways be less than a good thing.

The Mission and Ministry of the Church

Eighteen scales organize into four factors that give a rather full profile of what people feel is the appropriate mission and ministry of the church and, to some degree, how they feel about the way their church is presently carrying out its mission in specific forms of ministry.

Two of the four factors, The Church and Social Action (Factor Three) and Conscientious Individualism (Factor Four), concern people's beliefs, attitudes, and participation in matters having to do with the church and social issues. Issues of social justice raise the question of whether the church *as church* should (1) use its power as an institution in society to speak out univocally, (2) otherwise attempt to take action that will compel changes in the social structures to meet people's needs, and (3) provide social, economic, educational, and other types of justice for all people. Or, should the church provide a forum, counsel, and guidance that enables each member to do his part in bringing about social reform and justice (if that is presently lacking), while the church as church body refrains from becoming another power block in society attempting to change the system.

Factor Three, The Church and Social Action, is characterized by the following:

1. A general openness to change within the church itself;
2. Positive attitudes toward the church as church becoming involved in social issues;
3. Personal willingness and actual participation in programs and group action for broadening of civil rights and social justice;
4. Positive attitudes toward Lutheran clergymen taking leadership roles in social action; and
5. A tendency to view social issues as power struggles.

Negatively correlated with these characteristics are two

dimensions of prejudicial attitude, the first assessed by Scale 56, Social Distance from Persons Who Exhibit Radical Life Styles, and the second assessed by Scale 34, Generalized Prejudice. The profile of parochial school attendees regarding this factor is shown in Table 2.10.

TABLE 2.10

The Church and Social Action (Factor Three)

Parochial School Differences	Load	Scale	Dimension Title
	Positive		
	.69	78	Openness to Change Within the Church
	.66	65	Church Involvement in Social Issues
+ +	.61	12	The Church, Me, and Social Justice
+	.60	42	The Role of Pastors in Social Action
– –	.59	64	Power Orientation to Social Issues
	Negative		
– –	–.30	56	Social Distance – Radical Life Styles
+ + – –	–.32	34	Generalized Prejudice

Compared with persons who never attended parochial schools, those who reported some attendance are no more or less open to change within the church. Nor are they more or less inclined toward seeing the church as church body involved in a struggle for civil rights or involved in social issues. But they are more involved themselves in causes promoting social justice. They are somewhat more inclined to approve of their pastor's being involved in preaching, teaching, and discussing social issues as part of his ministry. And to a slight degree, they are more inclined to approve of pastors taking part in demonstrations or risking civil disobedience. Consistent with this, those who attended parochial schools tend to be significantly less prejudiced toward people whose life styles are very different from their own or who might be called radical (e. g., Communists, hippies, members of the John Birch Society or Students for a Democratic Society, homosexuals, ex-convicts, protestors against the draft). Although the parochially educated show more liberal attitudes and greater participation in causes of social justice which is characteristic of more family educated people in general. They may be that way because of a conviction that this is their Christian responsibility. This is shown in Table 2.11.

TABLE 2.11

Conscientious Individualism (Factor Four)

Parochial School Differences	Load	Scale	Dimension Title
	Positive		
+ +	.64	60	Individual Christian Responsibility
	.56	59	Social Utility of Christianity
	Negative		
−	−.52	62	Service Without Proclamation
	−.63	35	Pessimism
+	−.67	61	Image of Lutherans as Different

Factor Four is characterized by a belief that Christianity does have social value of social consequences, that is, a conviction that the church's teaching, preaching, and action has been and continues to be a force for good in society. It encompasses the conclusion that having become a Christian changes a person's attitudes and behavior. This factor also includes the conviction that every Christian has a responsibility to express his faith in actions that benefit his fellowmen, e. g., working for equal opportunity in housing and employment. This conviction is also coupled with an inclination to disagree that the church's mission is to serve the physical, emotional, and social needs of humanity without explicitly proclaiming the Gospel of salvation by grace through faith in Jesus Christ. It includes a general optimism, or at least not the pessimism that makes thought of taking action seem futile. Finally, Factor Four includes a view of Lutherans as somewhat distinct and different from other Christians for a variety of reasons including national heritage, personality tendencies, doctrine, and polity.

Those who attended parochial schools are much more convinced of their own individual Christian responsibilities and the responsibility of all Christians to live their faith for the sake of their fellowmen. They are somewhat inclined to see themselves (as Lutherans) as distinct from other Christians. And they are somewhat more inclined than those who never attended parochial schools to reject the idea that the Christian's calling is *only* to meet the needs of humanity without proclaiming the Gospel in direct preaching and teaching. All of this points to their Christian convictions as the source of their greater personal participation in the causes of civil rights, social justice, and the like.

It is very important to notice that although those who attended parochial schools are no more interested in the church's institutional involvement in social issues than their public school counterparts are, it is not because they carry no social concern for the welfare of their fellowmen. It is rather because they have a different view of how social concern should be expressed or of what kind of an expression will be most effective. This stance, more characteristic of those who have attended parochial schools, is also the stance of most Lutherans. Though they split about 50 – 50 on the question raised by Scale 65, still by a wide majority they want their pastors to call their attention to social issues and provide guidance and opportunity to discuss such issues. However, they do not want this guidance to come primarily from the pulpit. They prefer it in settings in which there can be open discussion. Nor do they wish simply to be told what they ought to do. Rather, they prefer to form their own judgments and come to their own conclusions about the best course of action to take to accomplish the most under the circumstances.

Lutherans have a tendency to equate parish life and family life. (See *A Study of Generations*, pages 165 – 6.) Therefore, in discussing the views those who have attended parochial school have of the mission and ministry of the church, we need to examine family and institutional loyalties. We need to ask: to what degree do persons identify with their parents or peers? Do they view their congregation and family as caring for other people or, by contrast, are they disappointed with the church? Table 2.12 summarizes the data on these questions. It reveals that those who attended parochial schools are somewhat less disappointed with the church than those who did not. It also shows that the parochially educated are more inclined to identify with their peers than are their public school counterparts. Yet they are no more or less inclined to identify with their own parents or to see their own families and congregations as caring effectively and considerately for themselves and other people.

TABLE 2.12
Reference Groups and Institutional Loyalty (Factor Eight)

Parochial School Differences	Load	Scale	Dimension Title
	Positive		
	.59	18	Identification with Parents
	.56	13	Family and Congregational Caring Life
	Negative		
+ +	−.52	63	Peer Orientation
−	−.55	27	Disappointment with the Church

Apparently parochial school attendees and graduates make finer distinctions and are more realistic in their perspectives and judgments. For example, they are significantly less inclined to view struggles for civil rights and other social issues as power struggles (see Scale 64, Table 2.10). There may indeed be power struggles involved. But to view such complex issues as really nothing more than simple power struggles is rather naive and simplistic. Therefore, that the parochially educated should be significantly less inclined to view social issues as power struggles is either an indication that they are able to view complex matters with a more critical, or at least with a different, eye than those who did not attend parochial schools.

Second, the parochially educated are somewhat more inclined to view Lutherans as distinctive or as different from other Christians and from other Protestant Christians (Table 2:11,

Scale 65). This may be an unfortunate discrimination. On the other hand, it may be evidence of heightened ability to make fine distinctions. It may indicate enough of a recognition of the distinctive character of Lutheran theology and perception and expression of the Gospel to know why one is a Lutheran rather than some other brand of Christian.

Third, the parochially educated tend to take neither a more nor less jaundiced view of their own parents, families, and congregations than do other members of the LCMS (Scales 18 and 13, Table 2.12). Apparently there is something about parochial school education that heightens one's identification with his peers. This may be related to the fact that for large numbers attendance at parochial schools has meant residence away from home and parents at a very young age. Nevertheless, here again is evidence that could be an indication of a more frank, realistic, finely discriminating eye. If so, it will be interesting to learn whether this characteristic is more a result of general level of education or an effect of parochial school attendance.

Table 2.13 merely indicates that attending parochial school is much more characteristic of those who were, so to speak, born into The Lutheran Church—Missouri Synod or who at least were not members of some other denomination before

TABLE 2.13
Prior Church Memberships (Factor Nine)

Parochial School Differences	Load	Scale	Dimension Title
	Positive		
— — —	.80	10	Prior Denominational Membership (Larger Bodies)
	.79	11	Prior Denominational Membership (Smaller Bodies)

joining. It also indicates that when people later join The Lutheran Church—Missouri Synod, they are more likely to have previously been members of one of the large mainline denominations than one of the smaller denominations or sects.

Personal Involvement and Service

Do their actions fit their beliefs, values, and attitudes? *A Study of Generations* found that among Lutherans the people who performed everyday acts of kindness that might be described as neighborliness and who go out of their way to support others in times of crises are also the ones who most actively talk about Jesus with other people. This kind of personal witness could be called personal evangelism. They are also the ones who tend to take the initiative on public issues and issues of churchwide concern. These four measures share in common the theme of personal service activities.

Table 2.14 shows that in everyday acts of kindness and special support at times of personal crisis, those who attended parochial schools show no more nor less care and concern for their neighbors than do those who did not attend. But those who attended parochial schools report that they more frequently engage in one-to-one witnessing about their faith, talking about their church, sharing Jesus Christ with others—activities often called personal evangelism. They also take the initiative in raising important issues in their communities or in the church significantly more frequently than do their counterparts who did not attend parochial schools.

TABLE 2.14
Personal Service Activities (Factor Five)

Parochial School Differences	Load	Scale	Dimension Title
		Positive	
	.86	22	Neighborliness
	.78	20	Supporting Others in Crises
+ +	.66	21	Personal Evangelism
+ +	.29	74	Personal Initiative on Church and Public Issues

Therefore, it is not surprising that on the average the parochial school educated are also much more highly involved in a broad variety of congregational activities, including both leadership and general participation as well as church attendance. They also show a higher level of giving of both money and time. Table 2.15 also indicates that although they are members of no more community organizations than church members who did not attend parochial schools, they are more involved in community and congregational service and action programs.

TABLE 2.15

Church and Community Involvement (Factor Six)

Parochial School Differences	Load	Scale	Dimension Title
	Positive		
+ + +	.69	40	Congregational Activity
	.63	45	Organizational Memberships
+ +	.61	47	Personal Involvement in Church and Community
+ +	.29	74	Personal Initiative on Church and Public Issues

The activities in which the parochially educated excel as shown in both Tables 2.14 and 2.15, are more characteristic of pastors than of lay people. When one looks at this portion of the profile of the parochially educated, one wonders if these differences may be due largely to the presence of significant numbers of clergy in the parochial school sample. The number of clergy in that sample is somewhat disproportionately high when compared with the ratio of pastors to lay people in the LCMS. The results of an investigation of this question will be discussed in Chapter 3.

One factor was characterized, not by measures of specific activities but rather by a general measure of orientation toward "doing" as a way of life. This was compared with a worldview that recognizes "being" or mere "existing as what one is" as the more important justification for Life. Factor Twelve was one of the most interesting of the weaker factors identified or formed by *A Study of Generations*.[5] First of all, Factor Twelve showed that Drug Culture Orientation was negatively correlated with Acceptance of Authority. This means that persons who are involved in or are prone to become involved in the drug culture either have difficulty accepting or simply reject authority to a greater degree than persons not involved in taking drugs and the way of life that surrounds it. Second, the positive end of Factor Twelve is characterized by two measures: Scale 51 which assesses degree or ease of accepting various sorts of individual or societal authority, and Scale 72 which assesses a person's tendency to value doing more than being.

Both inclination toward doing and easy acceptance of authority suggest control by persons outside oneself, external rather than internal control. Internalization of the Gospel, of course, would be the opposite of control by the power of the crowd or the immediate situation. It is interesting to note that the negative end of this factor includes the Gospel-oriented life. However, the strength with which any of the scales cluster about this theme is very weak indeed. Table 2.16 shows that ease of relating to or accepting authority is a different matter for the parochially educated. And once again it indicates a significant difference between those who report attending three years or less, those who reported 4−12 years of attendance, and those reporting no parochial school attendance. Those reporting 3 years or less find it harder to accept authority, and those who report 4−12 years attendance find it easier to accept authority than those who report no attendance at all. Whether those who

TABLE 2.16

Relationship to Authority (Factor Twelve)

Parochial School Differences	Load	Scale	Dimension Title
	Positive		
− − + +	.53	51	Acceptance of Authority
	.49	72	Orientation to "Doing" Influenced by the Church
	Negative		
+ +	−.21	70	Gospel-Oriented Life
+ −	−.31	29	Values of Self-Development
	−.35	73	Drug Culture Orientation

reported attending only 3 years or less might be less able to accept authority because of that brief attendance or whether they attended only 3 years or less because they were already sensitive to placing themselves under authority are questions about which we have no data.

Part of the weak cohesiveness of Factor Twelve is indicated by the fact that those who report the most parochial school attendance show significantly higher scores both on Scale 51, which has a positive factor loading of .53, and also Scale 70, which has a very light negative loading. A more consistent situation occurs for those who reported 3 years or less of parochial school attendance. Their scores on Scale 51, Acceptance of Authority, are significantly lower, while their scores on both Scales 70 and 29 are significantly higher.

This is the first time that such inconsistency in the profile of the parochially educated on a single factor has occurred. On the one hand, this emphasizes once more the apparent significant difference between persons who attended parochial school for only a few years and those who attended 7 – 12 years. On the other, it is likely a result of the relatively weak reliability of Scale 70, Gospel-Oriented Life (.50) and especially the weak consistency of Factor Twelve (eigenvalue 1.15 as compared with an eigenvalue of 9.61 for Factor One, The Heart of Lutheran Piety, in a factor analysis of the intercorrelations of the 64 parent scales).

Factor Thirteen concerned voting practices in national politics. The parochially educated characteristically voted no differently than their fellow members.

Summary

The ways in which the parochially educated tended to be different from others can be summarized in terms of four distinct types of believers identified after *A Study of Generations* had been written. The four types of believers differ consistently across a wide variety of characteristics, but most emphatically in their orientation to Law and Gospel. The four types, in terms

of orientation to Law and Gospel, are as follows: high Gospel –
low Law; high Gospel – high Law; low Gospel – low Law; and
low Gospel – high Law.

Those educated in parochial schools tend to differ significantly from those reporting no attendance by being much more
commonly types one and two; believers who are high Gospel –
low Law, or high Gospel – high Law. More precisely, those who
reported *more* years of parochial school attendance tend most
commonly to be more highly oriented to the Gospel and less
highly oriented to life under the Law. Those who reported *some*
parochial school attendance, particularly three years or less,
tend more characteristically to be rather highly oriented to both
Law and Gospel, that is, they tend to mix their Christian faith
with some degree of rigidity, legalism, or Pharisaism.

In all the following ways, people who reported the longest
parochial school attendance differ significantly from those who
never attended. These ways are characteristic of the believer
who has much more than an average awareness of Gospel and
is much less likely than the average to live life under the Law
(natural religion). They have profiles most like those of pastors.
They generally have high scores on all measures of basic Christian beliefs and are the more likely of all laymen to accept both
the divinity and humanity of Jesus as well as to be aware of God's
immanence. They are more knowledgeable about the Bible and
more likely to accept the exclusive truth claim of salvation
through Jesus Christ but to reject the heresy of claiming an exclusive channel of salvation through their own church. They are
more likely to reject salvation by works and utilitarian uses of
religion and the church. Most show some general signs of being
less alienated in that they are less disappointed with the church,
less self-oriented, and less peer-oriented. Likewise, they are less
prejudiced toward others and are less prone to use stereotypes
and scapegoats; at the same time they are more willing to forgive
others and to face both life and death with serenity and openness.
They support and take part in religious rituals without being
slavish to them. They are active in the church and community

but do not glorify the work ethic or work at all costs. They are willing to serve the church if and when they are called upon to do so and are more likely to exercise personal initiative in social affairs as well as in personal piety. Though they are more aware that the church has not been what it is called to be, they are unlikely to want the church to be primarily or exclusively a social reform agency at the expense of its clear proclamation of the Gospel of salvation by grace through faith. They exhibit an openness and neighborly spirit toward others who exhibit different life styles. They are typically the core or nuclear members of congregations, willing to teach Sunday and Bible school, faithful in their church support and personal piety, receptive to change, and have a life style centered in salvation through Christ.

There are a few ways in which the people who reported the most parochial school attendance are *not* generally like what is characteristic of the believer most highly oriented to the Gospel and least oriented to Law. Compared with the members who have never attended parochial school, the most parochially educated are no less likely to feel isolated, pessimistic, or powerless. They indicate no more sense of meaning and purpose in their lives and are no more ready to meet the world head on as it is rather than to try to escape or to wish it to be securely dependable. They are no more generally open, optimistic, or expectant. They don't feel that the church as church should be more involved in controversial issues. They are not less, but about equally as likely, to claim that they are neighborly, and they are on the average no more receptive to change in the church than are members who have never attended parochial school.

People who reported attending parochial schools for a relatively brief period of time, particularly 3 years or less, differ significantly from those who reported extensive attendance in the following ways. They are more likely to take a utopian view or have almost magical expectations of institutions including the church. They are more likely to believe that it is important to develop personally and to achieve; they are more inclined toward the work ethic, that is, to believe that work is always salutary and productive of personal gain. They are more likely to wish they could get away from it all or that they lived in the kind of world that is always predictable and dependable. And, in keeping with this latter tendency, they have greater need for maintaining existing structures and organizations and for keeping things from changing. They are more generally prejudiced and, if given the chance, would like to keep somewhat more socially distant from people who have different religious beliefs or who are of different races. When it comes to authority, they find it somewhat more difficult to accept authority when centered in individuals or expressed in the form of the norms of society.

Five of these tendencies of persons who report 3 years or less attendance in parochial schools fit what is characteristic of the believer who is highly oriented toward the Gospel at the same time that he is very much oriented to life as demand, expectation, conformity, or legalism. The five are utopianism, a Horatio Alger-like tendency to glorify work, an inclination to be prejudiced, and a need for unchanging structures in an unchanging and dependable world.

Some Additional Descriptive Detail

Information from isolated single items taken from a questionnaire is, of course, much less reliable than information from sets of items that form scales of known high reliability, such as that reported above. However, when information from single items fits the pattern of findings already discovered in the data from large numbers of highly reliable scales, then the information from single items is often very helpful in providing additional detail. The probability of its being reliable is enhanced by the fact that it is consistent with what has already been learned from very reliable measures.

Five hundred fifty-three of the 740 items in the *Study of Generations* questionnaire were included in the scales reported above. At least 100 more items provided demographic information. And of the approximately 90 items left, 33 provide some additional information related to four of the issues being investi-

71

gated in this study. They are issues number 5, 8, 11, and 12 as listed in Chapter 1.

Appendix A contains a table for each of these 33 isolated items offered as evidence in addition to the scales already cited above. In each case, the numbers of persons giving each of the response possibilities for the item are compared by number of years of parochial school they reported attending (again the five subgroups: none, 1−3 years, 4−6 years, 7−9 years, and 10−12 years). The chi-square statistic has been calculated for each table and is listed together with the probability of getting such a result purely by chance if, in fact, there were *no* significant relationship between number of years of parochial school attended and that particular item.

Better Lutherans?

The fifth issue in Chapter 1 raised the question of whether or not the parochially educated were indeed better Lutherans. The evidence cited so far points in that general direction. Five single items add additional weight to that possible conclusion (see items 478, 480, 481, 483, and 485 in Appendix A).

Four of the items are statements that are contrary to Christian faith and practice and to the stance taken by the majority of Lutherans. To all four statements the parochially educated tended to strongly disagree much more commonly than is the case for those who report never having attended parochial school or having attended for only a few years. The statements are:

A. (478) "It doesn't matter much what I believe as long as I lead a moral life";

B. (480) "Although I am a religious person, I refuse to let religious considerations influence my everyday affairs";

C. (483) "Although I believe in my religion, I feel there are many more important things in my life"; and

D. (485) "The only benefit one receives from prayer is psychological."

The fifth item (481) provides evidence that those who received no parochial education or only 3 years or less have a greater than expected tendency to attend worship no more than two to three times a month. Those who attended 4−6 years showed a greater than expected tendency to attend worship either once a week or less than once a month, while those who attended parochial school 7−9 years were unusually inclined to attend worship two to four times out of the average month. Those who attended parochial school the longest (10−12 years) were more inclined than might be expected to attend worship more than once a week.

Tackling the Real World?

Six isolated items relate to the eighth issue raised in Chapter 1: Are the parochially educated helped or hindered in coming to grips with the world? (See Items 197, 219, 282, 568, 569, and 574 in Appendix A.) On only one of these six items did the parochially educated demonstrate any difference from those who reported never having attended parochial schools. They showed no statistically significant differences (p < .01) in the number of friends they had who really care; in whether or not they had ever gone to a psychotherapist; in how happy they were with their daily work; or in whether they had or would ever ask for a raise or picket in a strike. In the one instance of what might be described as really coming to grips with the world (Item 568), those who reported most parochial school attendance tended more frequently also to report that they either had been compelled to, sometime in the past, or would bring a serious grievance to their boss if asked by others. Those who reported 6 years of attendance or less (including none) more frequently reported that they had brought a serious grievance either voluntarily or under pressure in the past, or that they had refused or would refuse to do so if asked.

As a whole, these six items provide no additional evidence that the parochially educated have been particularly helped in coming to grips with the world in its harsh reality.

More Christian Service?
The case has already been firmly established that the parochially educated are not particularly more neighborly or supportive in times of crisis, but they are more actively involved in personal evangelism, taking personal initiative on church and public issues, and in congregational leadership and activity. Thirteen separate items also bear on this issue (see Items 135, 142, 190, 531, 451, 549, 602, 604, 623, 624, 628, 645, and 674 in Appendix A). In summary, the parochially educated were found to place no higher value on social justice or fair treatment of all people, nor did they respond differently to statements such as:

"Concerns about caution have little place when the issue is one of social justice,"

"The church should never be silent over injustice in a local community," and

"My family seldom does anything about helping meet social problems."

In like manner, they reported that they no more frequently helped fellow students catch up on assignments, or gave old clothing, furniture, or other things to charitable organizations such as Goodwill, Salvation Army, or church sponsored secondhand stores (Items 190, 431, 451, 602, 645, and 674).

On the other hand, they reported significantly more frequently that they did listen to the problems of other people (friends or neighbors) and tried to give help or advice. They tended to belong to more service organizations and to give more money to their local congregations (though they were not giving more to nonchurch charities than they were four or five years ago). It is much more characteristic of the parochially educated to be teaching Sunday school now rather than to report that they once were teaching or that they never had taught (Items 628, 135, 142, 549, and 623).

Interestingly, though the four items mentioned above indicate they were not especially willing to take action for social justice, they did indicate that they would *not* be willing to support social injustice; they were much more inclined to respond "Not true" to the statement, "My family would support neighborhood efforts to keep out persons of other races." (Item 604)

Careful study of the tables for each of these items will indicate that in many cases the positive tendencies described above did not show themselves until seven or more years of parochial school attendance were reported and, in some cases, not until 10 – 12 years (for example, Sunday school teaching, as in Item 623). Nevertheless, these data from separate items were generally consistent with the pattern of greater Christian service on the part of the parochially educated, a pattern already established by the data from highly reliable scales.

More Stable and Satisfying Family Life?

Issue 12 raised in Chapter 1 questioned whether the parochially educated reported greater or less satisfaction with, and stability of, family life. The nine separate items that relate to this issue do not provide any evidence that the family life of those who attended parochial schools was any more satisfactory or stable than the nonparochial educated. They do provide some clues that those who attended parochial schools were more likely to come from homes in which both parents were very active in the church and where the religiousness of both parents is perceived as having been, at the time when the respondents attended parochial school, about as great as the respondents see their own religiousness now.

The parochially educated were not significantly different in the degree to which they expressed happiness or unhappiness about their family life (Item 280), nor was there significant difference in their present marital status, that is, the relative proportions of those who are single, married, divorced, or widowed (Item 732). No differences were found in the degree to which they reported being frequently ill, having serious difficulties in their home life during the past year, or being on welfare as individuals or a family. (Items 217, 218, and 220)

When asked to describe how active their fathers really were in the church during the respondent's youth, the degree of activity described tended to increase with the number of years of parochial school attendance (Item 721). The same was true, only more so, when they were asked to describe the degree of activity of their mothers in the church during that same period of time. (Item 722)

All in all, these data indicate that people who attend parochial schools tend to perceive their parents, and particularly their mothers, as active in the church. They also tend to perceive their parents as about as religious as they are now, or their fathers as somewhat more religious and their mothers as slightly less religious than they themselves at this time. Whether or not these parents actually were that way when the respondents were growing up, we do not know. We have no data on the church activity of parents or their "religiousness." All we have are data showing that the parochially educated tend to perceive their parents as having been as just described — and that that perception is different from the way those who never attended parochial school tend to perceive their parents.

When asked, however, to compare their own religiousness with that of their mothers, those who attended 10 — 12 years of parochial school were much more inclined than might be expected to see themselves as about the same or slightly more religious, while those who attended nine or less years, including none at all, showed a much greater tendency than might be expected to describe themselves as being either much more or much less religious (Item 550). When asked to make the same comparisons with their fathers, those who reported no attendance were significantly more inclined to describe themselves as some or much more religious, while those who attended parochial school any length of time were more inclined than would be expected to describe themselves as being the same or somewhat less religious than their fathers. (Item 551)

CHAPTER THREE

Was Attendance the Cause?

The Crucial Question

Does attending parochial school cause the differences between those who attended and those who did not? A cause and effect relationship is strongly suggested by the fact that as the number of years of parochial school attendance increases, the size of the differences between those who attended and those who did not seems to increase accordingly. Although it is necessary evidence, that increase alone is not sufficient for concluding cause and effect. Could not the parochially educated have become that different for other reasons? They surely could have if people who attended parochial schools also shared some other characteristic in common. This alternate explanation would be particularly true if they shared that characteristic in such a way that if they attended parochial school for a short time, they shared a small amount of that other characteristic, and if they attended parochial school for a long time, they tended to share a lot of that other characteristic.

Of the more than 100 pieces of descriptive information available to us for each person from *A Study of Generations* data, three were significantly correlated with number of years of parochial school attended. The three were education (the level of formal education ultimately attained), age, and whether or not a person was a clergyman. The probability is less than one in a million that the relationship between number of years of parochial school attended and eventual level of formal education, as shown in Table 3.1, occurred purely by chance.

Those who never attended parochial school have a greater than expected tendency to be high school graduates or to have had some college training. Of those who attended parochial

TABLE 3.1

Percentages of People Attaining Various Levels of Formal Education Compared by Number of Years of Parochial School Attended (Underlining indicates greater than expected percentages)

Highest Education Attained
Years Attended Parochial

Item 163: How much formal education have *you* had?

	8th	Some H. S. or Trade	H. S. Grad.	Some College	College Grad.	Some Prof.	Prof. Degree
None	6%	16%	41%	18%	7%	5%	6%
1 − 3	18%	20%	32%	13%	7%	4%	6%
4 − 6	1%	17%	36%	14%	8%	11%	13%
7 − 9	5%	16%	40%	12%	11%	6%	12%
10 − 12	2%	5%	14%	14%	7%	30%	30%
Average	8%	16%	33%	16%	8%	11%	13%

$x^2 = 164.894*$ $df = 24$ $p = < .000001$

* Calculated on the basis of the frequencies upon which these percentages are based

school 1 − 3 years, more than might be expected eventually only completed eighth grade or attended some high school or trade school. Of those who attended 4 − 6 years more than might be expected eventually graduated from high school, and many more than might have been expected of those who attended 7 − 9 years eventually graduated from high school or eventually graduated from college. To a much greater degree than might be expected those who attended 10 − 12 years of parochial school tended eventually to receive some professional training or a professional degree.

Table 3.2 shows beyond normal expectations that those who never attended parochial school tended to be in their twenties through forties; those who attended 1 − 3 years tended more to be in their teens, fifties, or sixties; those who attended 4 − 6 years tended more to be in their teens, twenties, and fifties; those who attended 7 − 9 years tended more to be in their teens, twenties, and thirties; and those who attended 10 − 12 years tended more to be in their thirties, fifties, and sixties.

TABLE 3.2

Number of People of Various Ages Compared by Number of Years of Parochial School Attended (Underlining indicates greater than expected frequencies)

Years Attended Parochial \ Age	Item 739: Age					
	15 – 19	20 – 29	30 – 39	40 – 49	50 – 59	60 – 65
None	139	192	215	246	139	37
1 – 3	59	49	59	64	78	25
4 – 6	16	23	11	11	15	2
7 – 9	23	28	33	28	14	3
10 – 12	4	8	13	6	9	4
Total	241	300	331	355	255	71

$x^2 = 55.2$ df = 20   p = .00006

That eventually becoming a clergyman is correlated with attending parochial school is clearly shown by the fact that only 3% of those who never attended became clergy; while 5% of Those who attended 1 – 3 years, 14% of those who attended 4 – 6 years, 11% of those who attended 7 – 9 years, and 49% of those who attended 10 – 12 years eventually became clergymen. (Table 1.2)

Any one or all three of these variables (education, age, and pastoral training and experience) are just as likely to be *the* cause of the parochially educated being different from those who never attended as parochial school attendance is. Fortunately, analysis of variance allows simultaneous examination of all four of these variables as possible causes of the ways in which the parochially educated differed from those who never attended. Of course, as mentioned in Chapter 1, with the cross-sectional data we have available, even such a sophisticated analysis cannot *prove* what caused the differences. However, if all alternative possibilities for which we have data can be ruled out, the odds favoring parochial school attendance as the likely cause will be increased.

Analytic Results

Two sets of three-way analyses of variance were performed across all 78 scales. In both sets of analyses, education, age, and length of parochial school attendance were the independent variables (the variables examined as possible "causes"), and the 78 scales assessing various beliefs, attitudes, values, opinions, and reported behaviors were the dependent variables (the variables considered to be "effects" of these possible causes). However, the entire sample, including both lay people and clergy, was used in the first set of analyses, while only lay people were included in the second set of analyses.[1]

The practical consequences of this analytic approach were as follows: In the first set of analyses, the effects of people's ages and their eventual levels of formal education were controlled (or removed); then the average scores of these subgroups of people who reported no parochial school attendance, $1 - 6$ years of parochial school attendance, and $7 - 12$ years of attendance, were compared again to see if the differences previously noted still persisted. (For a succinct description of what is involved in controlling for the effects of a particular variable, see pages 65 and 66 of *A Study of Generations*.) In the second analysis the effects of an additional variable were controlled. The effects of eventually becoming a clergyman as well as the effects of age and ultimate level of formal education were simultaneously controlled and the same investigation was carried out. The average scores for the three subgroups by length of parochial school attendance (none, $1 - 6$ years, and $7 - 12$ years) were examined and tested statistically to see if the differences that were observed previously, when these variables were not being controlled, still persisted.

In this way all four of the possibilities likely to be *the* cause of the parochially educated being different from those who never attended were examined. First, the consequences of people having been of certain ages and having received certain levels of formal education by 1970 were removed from the data; then the possible consequences of persons having been additionally trained and having additional experience as clergymen were also removed from the data; and finally the data were examined to see if there were still any differences between those who never attended parochial school and those who attended for varying lengths of time. One would expect that the remaining differences might well be fewer and lesser. Indeed, it could have been possible that no differences would have remained. Should that have occurred, there would have been no basis left from these data for proposing that attending parochial school might have had any consequences whatsoever. However, for any differences that did persist, the possibility that parochial school attendance might have caused those differences still would remain. The possibility would not have been disproved.

Table 3.3 summarizes the measures for which remaining differences between the parochially educated and those who never attended were just as great as they were when observed previously (before the effects of age, education, and clergy training were controlled).

TABLE 3.3

Scales for Which No Alternative Explanations Were Found for Differences

Scale No.	Scale Name	Apparent Difference	Remaining Difference
8	Biblical Knowledge	+ + +	+ + +
10	Prior Denominational Membership (Larger Denominations)	− − −	− − −
15	Salvation by Works	− −	− −
21	Personal Evangelism	+ +	+ +
41	Personal Piety	+ + +	+ + +
44	Fundamentalism-Liberalism	+	+

In Table 3.3 the same code of plus and minus signs is used as in the series of tables in Chapter 2. The column headed "Apparent Difference" indicates the size and kind of maximum differences in average standardized scale scores between any two of the three subgroups by length of parochial school attendance before age, education, and clergy experience were controlled. The column headed "Remaining Difference" indicates the size and kind of maximum differences between any two of the three subgroups by length of parochial school attendance after age, education, and clergy experience were controlled. Appendix B includes a detailed table for each of the scales mentioned in this chapter. For each scale the actual average scores for each of the three subgroups by length of parochial school attendance are reported for three stages of the analysis: (1) for all persons in the sample with no variables controlled, (2) with age and education controlled, and (3) with age, education, and clergy training and experience controlled. Careful examination of the information in Appendix B for each of the scales in Table 3.3 will show that progressively as more variables are controlled the average scores for each subgroup by length of parochial school attendance do not remain exactly the same. The subgroup average scores at the first stage of the analysis (controlled by age, education, and clergy training) are not identical, but they are relatively the same, that is, the kind and size of the maximum differences between any two subgroups are the same in terms of the plus and minus codes for differences used in Chapter 2.

Table 3.4 shows all measures for which the kind or magnitude, or both, of the differences between any two subgroups by length of attendance would change as a result of controlling for age, education, or clergy training. The variable or variables other than parochial school attendance found by analysis of variance to be responsible for the change are indicated with an "×" in the appropriate row under the column headed "Alternative Explanation."

The data in Table 3.4 should be interpreted as follows: Suppose, for example, that on a given scale the apparent difference is + + +, the remaining difference is +, and under "Alternative Explanation," "Age" is checked with an X. This would mean in terms of this particular measure that much of the great difference between those who never attended parochial school and those who did is most likely due to the age of the respondents rather than their parochial school attendance (age is positively correlated with amount of parochial school attendance). However, there is still a tendency for those who report some parochial school attendance to score slightly higher on the average on this measure than did those who never attended. This slight but significant difference cannot be accounted for by age, education, or additional experience as a pastor. It is therefore possibly, though still not necessarily, due to their attendance at parochial school.

TABLE 3.4

Scales for Which Alternative Explanations (Causes Other Than Parochial School Attendance) Were Found for Some or All of the Observed Differences Between Subgroups Reporting Varying Lengths of Parochial School Attendance.

Scale No.	Scale Name	Apparent Difference	Alternative Explanation			Remaining Difference
			Education	Age	Clergy Train.	
19	Religious Experience	+ +	X			+ + +
14	A Personal, Caring God	+		X		
29	Values of Self-Development	+ −		X		
69	Horatio Alger Orientation	+ −		X		
49	Anxiety over My Faith			X		−
60	Individual Christian Responsibility	+ +		X		
66	Emotional Certainty of Faith	+	X	X		
6	Divinity of Jesus	+ +	X	X		+ + +
36	Christian Utopianism	+ −	X	X		
54	Desire for Detachment from the World	+ + − −	X	X		
43	Need for Religious Absolutism	− −	X	X		
27	Disappointment with the Church	−	X	X		
57	Social Distance − Racial and Religious Groups	+ −	X	X		
42	The Role of Pastors in Social Action	+	X	X		
64	Power Orientation to Social Issues	− −	X	X		−
28	Transcendental Meaning in Life	+ +			X	+
58	Awareness of the Immanent Trinity	+ +			X	+
70	Gospel-Oriented Life	+ +			X	+
65	Church Involvement in Social Issues				X	− −
9	Biblical Ignorance	− −			X	−
61	Image of Lutherans as Different	+			X	
47	Personal Involvement	+ +			X	

No.	Scale	Apparent Difference				Remaining Difference
	in Church and Public Issues					
74	Personal Initiative on Church and Public Issues	+ +			X	
12	The Church, Me, and Social Justice	+ +	X		X	
63	Peer Orientation	+ +	X		X	+ −
71	(Positive) Attitudes Toward Life and Death	+ +		X	X	
62	Service Without Proclamation	−		X	X	Interaction
40	Congregational Activity	+ + +	X	X	X	
5	Humanity of Jesus	+ +	X	X	X	
16	The Exclusive Truth Claim of Christianity Exaggerated	+ +	X	X	X	+ + +
55	Family Education	+ +	X	X	X	
38	Traditional Family Ideology	+ +	X	X	X	+
52	Desire for a Dependable World	+ + − −	X	X	X	+
37	Need for Unchanging Structure	+ + − −	X	X	X	+
34	Generalized Prejudice	+ + − −	X	X	X	
56	Social Distance − Radical Life Styles	− −	X	X	X	
67	Self-Oriented Utilitarianism	− −	X	X	X	
51	Acceptance of Authority	− − + +	X	X	X	− +

Again in Table 3.4 the same code of plus and minus signs is used as in the series of tables in Chapter 2. Average standardized scores (mean for lay people = 50.0; standard deviation = 10.0) for all subgroups for all scales in Tables 3.3 and 3.4 at each of the three stages of the analyses are listed in Appendix B.

Again the column headed "Apparent Difference" shows the descriptive differences as found and reported in Chapter 2. The column headed "Remaining Difference" shows the differences that are still possibly due to parochial school attendance.

Pastoral experience and age are by far the more common alternative explanations, that is, causes other than parochial school attendance for the differences that occur on the average between the group that reported no parochial school attendance and the subgroups that reported varying lengths of attendance. The fact that large numbers of those who attended parochial schools some or all of the time between grades 1 and 12 eventually went on to become pastors seems to be the greatest cause of differences between the parochially educated and nonparochially educated other than actual parochial school attendance. Nevertheless, many significant differences still remain between the parochially educated and others for which this study has no explanation to offer other than the fact that they did attend parochial schools for part or all of the first 12 years of their education. We were not able to disprove the possibility.

In order to provide a much clearer picture of the remaining differences in a form comparable to the descriptive profile presented in Chapter 2, the same data as presented in Tables 3.3 and 3.4 will now be organized in terms of the factors of *A Study of Generations.*

Each of the next four tables will present one of the four groups of factors that were presented and discussed in Chapter 2: (1) beliefs and values, (2) Law orientation, (3) mission and ministry of the church, and (4) personal involvement and service. Each table will show, from left to right, the relative effects on differences associated with attending parochial schools, of controlling first for age and ultimate level of formal education received, and finally of controlling for age, education, and pastoral training-experience.

Table 3.5 shows that the following characteristics of the parochially educated should not be attributed to their parochial school attendance:

1. Slightly greater tendencies to believe in a personal, caring God;
2. Slightly more certainty of one's own faith:
3. Greater belief in the humanity of Jesus;
4. Greater openness and positive attitudes toward life and death generally; and
5. Slightly more or less inclination toward believing that one can arrive at a utopia by conversion of the world one-person-at-a-time, toward valuing self-development, toward work as always profitable, and toward detaching one's self from the world.

It also shows that less differences than are observed on the average concerning the following are *likely to be due to experiences that are a part of attending parochial schools:* placing high value on relationships with God and people, personally experiencing the presence of the triune God, and relating to other people in daily life out of a Gospel orientation.

TABLE 3.5

Differences in BELIEFS and VALUES Associated with Parochial School Attendance Controlled by Age, Education, and Pastoral Training-Experience (see Chapter 2 for code of plus and minus signs)

Parochial School Differences (No Correlated Variables Controlled)	Parochial School Differences (Effects of Age and Education Removed)	Parochial School Differences (Effects of Age, Education, and Pastoral Training-Experience Removed)	Load	Scale	Dimension Title
1. The Heart of Lutheran Piety (Factor One)					
			Positive		
+ +	+ +	+	.80	28	Transcendental Meaning in Life
+			.74	14	A Personal Caring God
+			.73	66	Emotional Certainty of Faith
+	+	+	.72	44	Fundamentalism-Liberalism
			.67	46	Importance of Christian Practices in My Life
+ +	+		.65	71	Attitude Toward Life and Death
+ + +	+ + +	+ + +	.55	41	Personal Piety
+ +	+ + +	+ + +	.54	19	Religious Experience
+ +	+ +	+	.52	58	Awareness of the Immanent Trinity
+ +	+ + +	+ + +	.52	6	Divinity of Jesus
+ +	Interaction	+ + +	.48	16	The Exclusive Truth Claim of Christianity Exaggerated
+ −			.44	36	Christian Utopianism
			Negative		
− −	− − −	− −	−.29	15	Salvation by Works
+ −			−.32	29	Values of Self-Development
2. More Specific Gospel-Orientation (Factor Fourteen)					
			Positive		
+ +	+ +	+	.44	70	Gospel-Oriented Life
+ +			.38	5	Humanity of Jesus
+ + +	+ + +	+ + +	.30	8	Biblical Knowledge

				Negative		
+ −				−.32	69	Horatio Alger Orientation

3. Meaning and Purpose in Life (Factor Seven)

				Positive		
				.70	68	Life Purpose
				.30	50	Acceptance of Middle-Class Norms
				Negative		
				−.68	17	Feelings of Isolation and Pressure
−			−	−.70	49	Anxiety over My Faith

4. Views of the Good Life (Factor Ten)

				Positive		
				.75	53	Desire for a Controllable World
+ + − −				.65	54	Desire for Detachment from the World
+ + − −		+	+	.58	52	Desire for a Dependable World

Observed differences that cannot rightly be attributed to any of the three potential causes other than parochial school attendance include:

1. A slight tendency toward more fundamental or more conservative theological stance;
2. Much greater involvement in practices of personal piety;
3. Less tendency to believe in salvation by works; and
4. Much greater knowledge of the Bible.

In a few cases, Table 3.5 indicates that parochial school attendance may be associated with even greater differences than are observed on the average between those who attended and those who did not:

1. Religious experience;
2. Belief in the divinity of Jesus, acceptance of the exclusive truth claim of Christianity;
3. Reduction of anxiety about one's faith; and
4. A slightly inflated desire for a dependable world.

It is important to note from Appendix B that the slightly increased differences in acknowledgement of religious experience (Scale 19), and belief both in the divinity of Jesus (Scale 6) and the exclusive truth claim of Christianity (Scale 16), occurred because controlling for age, education, and pastoral experience tended on the average to *lower* scores for those who reported *no* parochial school attendance. Removing the effects of age, education, and pastoral experience did not *increase* the average scores for those who reported the most parochial school attendance. Therefore, these controlled data show no increased tendency for the parochially educated to exaggerate the exclusive truth claim of Christianity or to claim unusual charismatic gifts such as speaking in tongues or healing by faith.

It is important to notice that the earlier observed differences in belief in the humanity of Jesus are no longer correlated with length of parochial school attendance. Yet the much greater tendencies to believe in the divinity of Jesus are still related to parochial school attendance. If the rest of the results of controlling for age, education, and pastoral training-experience are consistent with these findings, one could expect that results concerning Law orientation would include no reduction of prejudice and some slight tendencies toward need for structure or absolutism to be residually associated with parochial school attendance.

As a whole, Table 3.5 shows that most of the differences in beliefs and values exhibited on the average by those who attended parochial schools cannot be explained away on the basis of age, education, or later training or experience as clergy. On the basis of the data we have, it is still plausible, though not proved, that these differences in beliefs and values are due to parochial school attendance.

Unfortunately the same cannot be said for the variety of measures of Law orientation or misbelief. As originally observed, decreases in Law orientation were related to parochial school attendance. But, as shown in Table 3.6, most of the differences in average scores on misbelief scales disappear when they are controlled for age, education, and pastoral training and experience. In fact, the only differences that remain somewhat as they were originally observed are:

1. The tendencies toward less belief in salvation by works,
2. Slightly less Biblical ignorance,

3. Greater acceptance of the exclusive truth claim of Christianity that salvation is by grace through faith in Jesus Christ alone and that there is one true but not visibly identifiable church.

Notice that the tendency toward acceptance of the exclusive truth claim of Christianity is slightly increased when controlled for age, education, and clergy training. This is not an adverse finding. It is only an indication that on the average the beliefs of those who did not attend parochial school would be less conservative than originally observed if controlled for age, education, and pastoral experience.

TABLE 3.6

**Differences in LAW ORIENTATION Associated with Parochial School
Attendance Controlled by Age, Education, and Pastoral Training-
Experience (see Chapter 2 for code of plus and minus signs)**

Parochial School Differences (No Correlated Variables Controlled)	Parochial School Differences (Effects of Age and Education Removed)	Parochial School Differences (Effects of Age, Education, and Pastoral Training-Experience Removed)	Load	Scale	Dimension Title
1. Misbelief or Life Under the Law (Factor Two)					
			Positive		
+ + − −		+	.76	37	Need for Unchanging Structure
− −			.70	43	Need for Religious Absolutism
+ + − −	− −		.69	34	Generalized Prejudice
− −	−		.69	56	Social Distance – Radical Life Styles
+ −			.65	57	Social Distance – Racial and Religious Groups
− −	−		.53	67	Self-Oriented Utilitarianism
+ +	Interaction	+ + +	.49	16	The Exclusive Truth Claim of Christianity Exaggerated
			.47	26	Mutual Support Among Church, Society and Ind.
+ −			.44	36	Christian Utopianism
− −	− − −	− −	.38	15	Salvation by Works
+ −			.36	69	Horatio Alger Orientation
			.32	35	Pessimism

			Negative		
+			−.34	42	The Role of Pastors in Social Action
	− −		−.35	65	Church Involvement in Social Issues
+ +			−.36	5	Humanity of Jesus
+ +	Interaction		−.42	55	Family Education Level

2. Self-Orientation or Natural Religion (Factor Eleven)

			Positive		
− −	− −	−	.54	9	Biblical Ignorance
			.42	23	Questionable Personal Activities
+ −			.36	29	Values of Self-Development
+ −	− − −	− −	.33	15	Salvation by Works

Scale 16 (the Exclusive Truth Claim of Christianity Exaggerated) was one of the scales upon which Lutheran Church — Missouri Synod lay people on the average scored higher than lay people from the other two Lutheran bodies. On this scale LCMS clergy scored significantly higher even than LCMS lay people (raw scores of 71.5 versus 66.4). Therefore, a special analysis of variance was conducted concerning it. In this analysis, instead of controlling for pastoral training and experience by removing the clergy from the sample, both clergy and lay people were left in the sample. The independent variables analyzed were age, length of parochial school attendance, and whether a person was a layman or a pastor. The results showed a slight interaction (p=.018) between clergy/lay status and length of parochial school attendance. Careful examination of the interaction showed that for lay people attending parochial school was associated with a slight increase in acceptance of the exclusive truth claim of Christianity. By contrast, for clergy parochial school attendance was associated with a slight decrease in acceptance of the exclusive truth claim of Christianity. These findings suggest that when compared with the overall tendency for lay people to underemphasize the exclusive truth claim of Christianity and for clergy of the LCMS possibly to exaggerate it, the effects of attending parochial school may generally be ameliorative. That is, parochial school attendance tends to remove some of the underemphasis among lay people and to remove some of the exaggeration among clergy.

As anticipated from the findings concerning beliefs in the divinity and humanity of Jesus, the earlier observed differences in prejudice did disappear. A slight tendency toward need for unchanging structure showed up, possibly attributable to parochial school attendance. The definite tendency to disfavor church involvement in social issues (Scale 65) is consistent with these findings, especially when viewed in light of the beliefs and values found to be generally associated with each other among Lutherans as a whole in *A Study of Generations*.

More careful examination of the scores for Scales 37 and 38 (see Appendix B) shed some light on the nature of the slight tendency toward need for unchanging structure that is residually associated with parochial school attendance. Scale 37, Need for Unchanging Structure, is made up of two subscales: Scale 39, Nonchange Orientation, and Scale 38, Traditional Family Orientation. Since only one of these two subscales reflects differences, Scale 37 as a whole doesn't quite show a significant difference between the parochially educated and others. But the subscale difference is particularly interesting. Scale 39, Nonchange Orientation, shows no differences between the parochially educated and others. Scale 38, Traditional Family Orientation, shows great differences even after controlling for age, education, and clergy training. The need for unchanging structure that is possibly attributable to parochial school attendance is a definite inclination toward traditional family orientation. Traditional family orientation, as measured by Scale 38, consists chiefly of a tendency toward male supremacy, a strict delineation of male and female roles in family life, and an emphasis on the need for children to conform and to be kept somewhat uninformed about such "adult" things as sex. Order and male authoritarianism predominate in this view of what is proper in family life.

As a whole, regarding Law orientation, it is possible that parochial school attendance significantly decreases natural religion or eradicates natural man's ignorance concerning his own sinful separation from God and men. It apparently destroys some of man's natural confidence in his own ability to save himself by performing in ways thought to be pleasing to God. Nevertheless, the data still offer clues that parochial education may foster at least some slight mixture of legalism in with the life in the Gospel.

Most of the earlier observed differences in measures concerning mission and ministry of the church can be attributed to age, education, and pastoral experience. Table 3.7 shows that only four out of the 11 previously observed differences were

TABLE 3.7

Differences in MISSION AND MINISTRY OF THE CHURCH Associated with Parochial School Attendance Controlled by Age, Education, and Pastoral Training-Experience (see Chapter 2 for code of plus and minus signs)

Parochial School Differences (No Correlated Variables Controlled)	Parochial School Differences (Effects of Age and Education Removed)	Parochial School Differences (Effects of Age, Education, and Pastoral Training-Experience Removed)	Load	Scale	Dimension Title
1. The Church and Social Action (Factor Three)					
			Positive		
			.69	78	Openness to Change Within the Church
		− −	.66	65	Church Involvement in Social Issues
+ +	+		.61	12	The Church, Men, and Social Justice
+			.60	42	The Role of Pastors in Social Action
− −	−	−	.59	64	Power Orientation to Social Issues
			Negative		
− −	−		−.30	56	Social Distance – Radical Life Styles
+ + − −	− −		−.32	34	Generalized Prejudice
2. Conscientious Individualism (Factor Four)					
			Positive		
+ +			.64	60	Individual Christian Responsibility
			.56	59	Social Utility of Christianity

			Negative		
−		Interaction	−.52	62	Service Without Proclamation
			−.63	35	Pessimism
+	+		−.67	61	Image of Lutherans as Different

3. Reference Groups and Institutional Loyalty (Factor Eight)

			Positive		
			.59	18	Identification with Parents
			.56	13	Family and Congregational Caring Life
			Negative		
+ +	+ +	+ −	−.52	63	Peer Orientation
−			−.55	27	Disappointment with the Church

4. Prior Church Memberships (Factor Nine)

			Positive		
− − −	− − −	− − −	.80	10	Prior Denominational Membership (Larger Bodies)
			.79	11	Prior Denominational Membership (Smaller Bodies)

maintained to any significant degree, and one new difference developed after controlling for the other three potential causes. Of these five remaining differences, the largest, having to do with prior denominational membership, is, of course, not even potentially an effect.

That the parochially educated should be slightly less inclined to view social issues primarily as power struggles (Scale 64) may well indicate, as suggested in Chapter 2, greater powers of discrimination or sophistication of thought. However, some items in Scale 64 shed a different light on what may be involved here. These additional items in Scale 64 show a tendency for the parochially educated to say that —

1) they do not feel that the doctrines of the church need to grow and to develop to keep up with the needs of the time;

2) their own understanding of the central doctrines of the church has not changed considerably during the last several years;

3) they do not believe that there is a generation gap today,

4) they would not tend to devote much of their time to reform movements if they were to follow their deepest convictions; and

5) they do not necessarily believe that the most important issues in the world today are issues of social justice.

These tendencies can be viewed on the one hand as indication of maturity of thought and conviction. On the other hand, they can be viewed as a tendency toward rigidity or inflexibility. In either case they fit the findings already discussed and shown in Table 3.6 regarding need for unchanging structures, particularly, in relation to family life. They are also consistent with the findings regarding Scale 65. Thus, one might conclude that the parochially educated are less inclined to place great importance on issues of social justice and to feel that the church should be heavily involved in such issues.

The other two differences in perspective on the mission and ministry of the church that are not attributable to age, education, or being a clergyman, are rather complex. Those who received less parochial education are slightly more inclined to be peer oriented than those who attended parochial schools longer. The latter are slightly less inclined to take their cues for norms and behaviors only from their own age group or those they view as their own contemporaries and peers. But which is cause and which is effect is an open question. Since one of the characteristics of peer-oriented youth in general is that they tend to be less academically oriented, one could build a reasonable case for the claim that being more peer-oriented would lead to attending parochial schools less long. On the other hand, a reasonable case could also be built for claiming that the isolation of the parochial school educational experience could at first develop a greater tendency toward group spirit and peer orientation; but as the parochial school experience continued, greater openness to broader contacts and more outside influences might reasonably develop as one became more comfortable in the parochial school setting. We simply do not know the dynamics of this slight but definite relationship between peer orientation and differing lengths of parochial school attendance.

The scores that people receive for Scale 62 shows an interaction between the effects of the total amount of formal education received and length of parochial school attendance. Scale 62 measures a person's tendency to favor the church's serving the total needs of persons without placing any special emphasis on proclaiming the Gospel of Jesus Christ to them. (For a brief basic explanation of interaction, see *A Study of Generations*, pages 65 – 67.) Figure 3.1 shows this interaction in its full complexity. No general pattern is apparent, but the highest and lowest scores are worth careful examination.

Figure 3.1

Average Scores (adjusted for age) of Lay People for Scale 62, Service Without Proclamation, Showing the Interaction of Total Formal Education Received (by Quartiles)* with Length of Parochial School Attendance

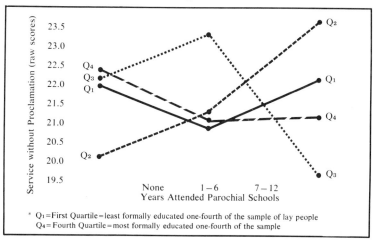

* Q₁=First Quartile=least formally educated one-fourth of the sample of lay people
Q₄= Fourth Quartile=most formally educated one-fourth of the sample

On the average, those in the second quartile of formal education would not have received a college degree. Even with 7 – 12 years of parochial school, they show the highest tendency toward believing the church's mission is to provide service without direct proclamation of the Gospel. By contrast, those in the third quartile on the average probably received a college education beyond the 12 years of parochial school attendance. They tend to be the least inclined toward seeing the church provide service without proclamation. These findings seem to contradict ideal outcomes. However, closer examination reveals that the difference between average scores for Quartiles 2 and 3 (for 7 – 12 years of parochial school attendance) is only the difference between *disagreeing* with all of the items in the scale (Q 2) and *strongly* disagreeing with one item while only disagreeing with the rest. (Q 3). Interaction generally covers only a range of scores that represents a difference in degree of rejection of service without proclamation of the Gospel.

As a whole, the differences here manifested by the parochially educated that cannot be explained by their age, ultimate level of education, or possible pastoral training and experience are minimal. Those that do persist, that are therefore possibly a result of parochial school attendance, include a perspective that the church's mission and ministry is something other than to become immersed in social issues. There are hints in the data that the parochially educated would at least want to be sure that such involvement in social issues would be accompanied by – if not superseded by – a clear verbal proclamation of the Gospel.

Of the eight differences in personal activities observed earlier to be associated with parochial school attendance, only three cannot be explained by other possible causes. The differences of involvement in practices of personal evangelism persist to about the same degree. The inclination toward acceptance of authority and toward communicating Gospel in one's interpersonal interactions remain but are not quite as strong. These remaining differences are shown in Table 3.8.

Talking regularly about Jesus Christ and the church with one's family and others seems to be action persistently associated with parochial school attendance. On the basis of differences measured by Scale 70, Gospel-Oriented Life, one could also expect the parochially educated to be slightly more ready to deal forthrightly with difficult situations and to approach others in

TABLE 3.8

Differences in Personal Involvement and Service Associated with Parochial School Attendance Controlled by Age, Education, and Pastoral Training-Experience (see Chapter 2 for code of plus and minus signs)

Parochial School Differences (No Correlated Variables Controlled)	Parochial School Differences (Effects of Age and Education Removed)	Parochial School Differences (Effects of Age, Education, and Pastoral Training-Experience Removed)	Load	Scale	Dimension Title
1. Personal Activities (Factor Five)					
			Positive		
			.86	22	Neighborliness
			.78	20	Supporting Others in Crises
+ +	Interaction	+ +	.66	21	Personal Evangelism
+ +	+ +		.29	74	Personal Initiative on Church and Public Issues
2. Church and Community Involvement (Factor Six)					
			Positive		
+ + +	+ + +		.69	40	Congregational Activity
			.63	45	Organizational Member-ships
+ +	+ +		.61	47	Personal Involvement in Church and Community
+ +	+ +		.29	74	Personal Initiative on Church and Public Issues
3. Relationship to Authority (Factor Twelve)					
			Positive		
− − + +	+	− +	.53	51	Acceptance of Authority
			.49	72	Orientation to "Doing" Influenced by the Church
			Negative		
+ +	+ +	+	−.21	70	Gospel-Oriented Life
+ −			−.31	29	Values of Self-Development
			−.35	73	Drug Culture Orientation

these situations directly (one-to-one) with an openness and desire to be forgiving. The slight tendency for those who attended parochial schools longest to be more accepting of authority as lodged in individuals and society in general is not of such magnitude that it could be interpreted as a docility or saccharine meekness. Scale 51, Acceptance of Authority, may indicate no more than a healthy respect for order and the rights of others.

The Trend Persists

The most telling evidence in favor of the remaining differences actually being due to parochial school attendance is the fact that the differences that persist generally tend to increase with length of parochial school attendance in the same manner as they did when first observed (see Appendix B, Scales 6, 8, 9, 10, 15, 16, 19, 21, 28, 37, 38, 41, 44, 51, 52, 58, 63, 64, 70). Any variable that might be cited as an alternative or better explanation for the persistent differences would have to be highly positively correlated with length of parochial school attendance. It would have to cause the differences in beliefs and values characteristic of the parochially educated at the same time that it varied consistently with the *number of years* of parochial school attended. Or it would have to be some kind of selection factor that would simultaneously cause parents to elect to send their children to parochial schools for the number of years proportionate to the degree that it caused changes in the beliefs and values of their children.

Therefore, if asked, "Is it likely that if controlled for the possible effects of other variables that might somehow be correlated with parochial school attendance, would these differences associated with length of parochial school attendance disappear?" I would tend to speculate that it could happen, but that it would be quite unlikely. In fact, the odds are increasingly in favor of parochial school attendance as the cause of the persistent differences since age, education, and pastoral experience were not found to account for all of the observed differences. Nevertheless, the inability of this research to disconfirm length of parochial school attendance as the possible cause of significant differences in beliefs, values, and personal practices is not sufficient evidence to confirm or prove that parochial school attendance is *the* cause or even *a* cause. However, this research does provide considerable necessary, but not sufficient, evidence to support that claim. The most that can be said from this research is that, despite attempts to muster sufficient evidence to the contrary from all the data from *A Study of Generations*, it is possible, in fact quite probable, that the residual differences associated with varying lengths of parochial school attendance were results of parochial school attendance. Ability to disprove does not confirm. It only leaves the possibility open.

In summary, when controlled for the possible effects of age, level of education ultimately achieved, and pastoral training and experience, length of parochial school attendance is still definitely correlated with the following:

1. A greater knowledge of the Bible,
2. More consistent affirmation of traditional Christian beliefs and values that emphasize the importance of relationships with God and other people,
3. Increased or more consistent practices of personal piety,
4. Less Pelagianism,
5. Increased personal evangelism, and
6. Less anxiety over personal faith and relationships with God.

In addition, parochially educated clergy show slightly less tendency toward exaggeration of the truth claim of Christianity and denominational exclusivism, while laity show slightly less tendency toward liberal beliefs when parochially educated.

With these generally positive findings are some slight indications of possible problem areas. When the effects of correlated sources of variation have been removed, length of parochial school attendance is still associated with slightly increased tendencies toward:

1. Male authoritarianism and need for unchanging family structures;
2. Less desire for the church to be involved in social issues; and
3. Slightly increased acceptance of authority and increased peer orientation among those attending just three years.

Further Support for Longer Attendance

So far we have been considering only length of attendance. The four most popular attendance patterns — grades 1 – 6, 1 – 9, 7 – 9, and graduation — were also contrasted with each other and with no attendance, while age and pastoral experience were controlled.

Some results paralleled what has already been reported. Table 3.9 shows that, with one exception, attendance in grades 1 – 9 and attendance long enough to graduate were the only two popular patterns that differed significantly from no attendance at all for nine of the seventeen scales for which simple, systematic, significant differences were found. (The heavy vertical lines in Table 3.9 separate groups which differ significantly from each other, scale by scale. For instance, for the first six measures

TABLE 3.9

Scales on Which Average Scores for Laymen Differ Significantly by Popular Patterns of Attendance Arranged Sequentially from Least to Greatest Number of Years Attended (Scores Standardized for LCMS Laymen with Average = 50.0 and the Standard Deviation = 10.0)

| Scale | Title | Popular Patterns of Attendance | | | | | Prob-ability * |
		None	Grades 7 – 9	Grades 1 – 6	Grades 1 – 9	Grad-uation	
8	Biblical Knowledge	49.6	49.8	49.3	54.0	54.4	< .0001
9	Biblical Ignorance	50.9	51.8	50.7	48.6	47.8	< .01
15	Salvation by Works	50.6	52.0	50.9	47.7	45.3	< .0001
41	Practices of Personal Piety	49.9	50.9	51.4	52.9	55.8	< .0001
58	Belief in the Immanent Trinity	48.8	49.7	48.2	51.8	51.8	< .01
64	Power Orientation Towards Social Issues	48.5	50.2	49.1	46.9	45.6	< .01
40	Congregational Activity	49.6	50.9	51.0	51.2	53.9	< .01
21	Personal Evangelism	49.6	50.3	51.9	51.8	54.3	< .0001
16	Exclusive Truth Claim of Christianity	49.9	53.1	52.4	53.7	57.0	< .0001

(Heavy verticle lines between columns separate groups that are significantly different.)
* See chapter note 2.

100

listed, those who attended only grades 7 − 9 or a portion thereof, or grades 1 − 6 or a portion thereof, did not differ significantly from those who attended not at all; but those who attended grades 1 − 9 or who attended long enough to graduate did differ significantly from those who had never attended or attended only grades 7 − 9 or 1 − 6.) Table 3.9 illustrates once again what has already been reported: more years of attendance are associated with greater differences. To put it a little more precisely, with the exception of Scale 16, none of the other eight scales showed any differences until *at least* 9 years of parochial school were involved. And Congregational Activity (Scale 40) and Personal Evangelism (Scale 21) showed no differences until *more than* 9 years of attendance. That length of attendance rather than attendance in the upper grades is associated with the differences is demonstrated by the fact that average scores for attendance in grades 7 − 9 only were consistently different from average scores for those attending grades 1 − 9.

Notice also that the average standard scores reported in Table 3.9 vary in the same direction and by approximately the same magnitude as previously reported when length of attendance without reference to specific grades was all that was being compared. In this case, length of attendance (0, 3, 6, 9, and 12 years) is confounded with the particular grade groups that happen to be the most popular attendance spans (none, 7 − 9, 1 − 6, 1 − 9, and graduation). Therefore, Table 3.9, organized by popular attendance patterns shows that generally members of The Lutheran Church − Missouri Synod show increasing amounts of these positive characteristics in correlation with length of parochial school attendance.

However, when analyzed in terms of popular attendance patterns, three other scales showed a pattern of variation *not* related to length of attendance. Table 3.10 gives instances where values, beliefs, and reported actions tended to differ depending not upon length of attendance but upon whether attendance was in the lower or upper grades. In these instances the upper grades are apparently superior.

TABLE 3.10

Scales for Which Only Popular Patterns of Attendance in the Upper
Grades Show Significant Differences on the Average from No Attendance
(Average Standardized Score for LCMS Lay People
= 50.0 With Standard Deviation = 10.0)

Scale	Title	None	Grades 1 – 6	Grades 7 – 9	Grades 1 – 9	Grad- uation	Prob- ability*
		Popular Patterns of Attendance					
28	Transcen- dental Meaning in Life	49.5	49.6	51.1	52.4	52.5	.001
44	Fundamen- talism – Liberalism	49.9	50.0	52.0	52.4	52.5	.01
70	Gospel Ori- entation to Life	50.9	49.8	52.9	51.7	54.2	.01

(Heavy vertical lines between columns separate groups that are significantly different.)
* See chapter note 2.

Table 3.11 provides additional evidence that certain beliefs
and attitudes are related more to the grade level attended than
to the length of attendance. This is particularly suggested by
the data from a few scales for those attending only grades 7 – 9.
Attention is drawn even more forcefully to grades 7 – 9 alone
when one notices that tendencies to want to get away from it all
(Scale 54) are strongest on the average for those who attended
only grades 7 – 9 *and least among those who went on to graduate
at grade 12.*

Notice furthermore that with the exception of Scale 55, all
the measures reported in Table 3.11 assess characteristics that
are potentially negative or deleterious. Horatio Alger Orientation is a set of beliefs and attitudes that amount to confidence
in inerrant virtues and positive consequences of hard work,
some tendencies to resist change, and an expressed willingness
to exert authority commensurate with one's position. Traditional
Family Ideology has been discussed earlier as a form of need
for male authoritarianism and rigid family roles and structures.
Desire for Detachment from the World is a set of values that
includes a desire to get away from it all and to live in isolation,
while Scale 57 is a measure of desire to keep from associating
socially with people who are of different races or religions.

TABLE 3.11

Scales Showing Potentially Negative Characteristic Differences Associated with Either Only Three Years of Attendance or Attendance Only During Grades 7−9
(Average Standardized Score for LCMS Lay People = 50.0 With Standard Deviation = 10.0)

		Popular Patterns of Attendance					
Scale	Title	Grades 7−9	None	Grades 1−6	Grades 1−9	Graduation	Probability*
69	Horatio Alger Orientation	52.3	49.3	49.4	49.7	48.7	< .01
38	Traditional Family Ideology	53.0	50.0	51.5	50.1	51.8	< .01
54	Desire for Detachment From the World	52.5	49.6	51.2	49.8	48.2	< .01
55	Family Level of Education	44.8	48.3	48.0	47.7	50.2	< .001
57	Social Distance: Race and Religion	52.6	50.1	51.8	50.7	52.4	< .01

(Heavy vertical lines between columns separate groups that are significantly different.)
* See chapter note 2.

Notice, finally, that regarding the Horatio Alger Orientation and Traditional Family Ideology, only the group attending grades 7−9 differed significantly from all others, including those who never attended. By contrast, both those who attended only grades 7−9 and those who graduated differed significantly from the rest in their desire for detachment from the world. The junior high attendees on the average showed the *greatest* desire to get away from it all, while the graduates showed the *least* desire.

This latter situation emphasizes the possibility that there was something additionally distinctive about those who attended only sometime during grades 7−9. Family Level of Education, Scale 55, followed the same pattern though inversely, that is, those attending only grades 7−9 showed on the average the lowest levels of family education, while those who graduated showed on the average the highest. Therefore, Family Level of Education may be confounding what appear to be effects of parochial school attendance only at grades 7−9. In *A Study of Gen-*

erations slightly higher scores on Horatio Alger Orientation, Traditional Family Ideology, and Desire for Detachment from the World were associated with lower levels of education. This was also the case with desire to keep socially distant from persons of other races and religions, Scale 57. The one place, however, where the hypothesis that the significant differences apparently related to attendance at grades 7−9 were actually caused by the differences in general educational achievement does not hold, is the case of Scale 57. The two groups that both differ by being both significantly more inclined toward remaining socially distant are the junior high attendees who on the average have the *lowest* level of family education *and* graduates who on the average have the *highest* level of family education.

The data in Table 3.11 show that certain legalistic and somewhat negative attitudes are related to attending only grades 7−9 or portions of them, or are related to attending three years or less. The latter is particularly true if those three years are during grades 7−9. There is reasonable evidence to conclude that this relationship is reinforced, if not partly caused, by the lower levels of ultimate educational achievement that accompany attendance only during grades 7−9. The question that still remains very open is whether the distinctive characteristic is attendance during grades 7−9 or attendance during *any* three years or less.

Prior denominational membership is one additional, potentially-confounding variable that can be ruled out as underlying the relationship between attendance during grades 7−9 and certain negative characteristics. Analysis of average scores for these same groups on Scale 10, a measure of previous membership in large denominations, revealed that those who attended grades 1−9, or only grades 7−9, are much less likely previously to have belonged to another denomination. Those who never attended parochial school are more likely to have been members of another denomination sometime in the past (actual average standardized scores in sequential order are as follows: grades

$1 - 9 = 46.2$, grades $7 - 9 = 47.4$, graduation $= 48.5$, grades $1 - 6$ $= 49.8$, and none $= 51.5$).

Is There a Best Time to Attend?

The data presented so far have related the 78 measures to two parochial school variables: "length of parochial school attendance" and "popular patterns of attendance." The third parochial school variable described in Chapter 1 was called "grades attended." In analyses concerning which grades were attended, five subgroups of persons were compared again on all 78 measures. The persons included in these comparisons all attended only three years or less of parochial school, but they attended at different grade levels. They attended some or all of the three grades in one of the following five groupings: none, grades $1 - 3$, grades $4 - 6$, grades $7 - 9$, and grades $10 - 12$.

Data presented so far have shown that:

1. Longer parochial school attendance is associated with greater differences, with most differences beginning to show only after 7 to 9 years of attendance; and

2. Four desirable and four undesirable differences were associated with 3 years of attendance; three out of the four desirable differences were apparently due more to the grade levels attended during those 3 years than the fact of 3 years of attendance per se.

These findings promote the maxim, "If you're going to attend at all, don't limit it to a few years; attend all 12!" Therefore, persons who attended only certain groups of three grades each were compared not primarily because there might be some particular advantage in attending only 3 years. Rather, a comparison of persons who never attended with persons who attended each of four three-grade groupings should show the differential effects of each three-grade interval: $1 - 3$, $4 - 6$, $7 - 9$, and $10 - 12$.

In summary, comparisons by three-grade intervals revealed the following on the average:

1. Those who attended only grades $1 - 3$ were not signifi-

cantly different on any of the measures from those who never attended.

2. Those who attended grade 4 or above differed significantly on three characteristics (two desirable characteristics and one undesirable).

3. Those who attended grade 7 or above differed significantly on two desirable and two undesirable characteristics.

4. Those attending grade 10 or above differed on one desirable and one undesirable characteristic.

5. Those who attended only grades 7, 8, or 9 differed significantly on one undesirable characteristic plus two rather neutral descriptors (Education and Prior Membership).

Age and the possible effects of clergy training and experience were controlled in all of these comparisons by grades attended.

Table 3.12 summarizes the desirable characteristics associated with attendance at specific grade levels.

TABLE 3.12

Desirable Beliefs, Attitudes, and Reported Behaviors That on the Average Varied Systematically Depending on the Three Grades Attended (Average Standardized Score for LCMS Lay People = 50.0 With Standard Deviation = 10.0)

Scale	Title	None	Grades 1–3	Grades 4–6	Grades 7–9	Grades 10–12	Prob-ability*
16	The Exclusive Truth Claim of Christianity	49.9	50.7	54.5	53.3	53.4	< .0001
51	Acceptance of Authority	49.7	50.3	46.4	46.2	45.8	< .0001
19	Religious Experience	48.2	51.1	49.8	51.6	53.6	< .0001
68	Life Purpose	51.0	50.9	46.9	52.6	52.3	< .01
21	Personal Evangelism	49.4	52.2	51.2	50.0	55.5	< .001

(Heavy vertical lines between columns separate groups that are significantly different.)
* See chapter note 2.

If these data were not accompanied by other preceding data that clearly evidenced the apparent cumulative effects of more years of attendance, one might be tempted to conclude that attending the first 3 years of parochial school is obviously without consequence. Such a conclusion, of course, does not follow from these data. Rather, one can appropriately conclude that attendance *only* in the first three grades apparently has no effects that can be detected by the 78 measures from *A Study of Generations*. However, on the basis of data concerning length of attendance and popular attendance patterns, it is reasonable to assume that attendance during the first three grades does have a cumulative effect *when added to attendance in later grades.* If this were *not* the case, one would expect that the data in Table 3.12 would, for grades 4 – 6 and above, show all of the differences previously found to be associated with more than 3 years of parochial school attendance; but the data do not.

Table 3.13 shows the specific undesirable differences that are associated with attendance above grade four.

TABLE 3.13

Undesirable Beliefs and Attitudes Systematically Associated with up to 3 Yers of Attendance, Depending on the Three Grades Attended (Average Standardized Score for LCMS Lay People = 50.0 With Standard Deviation = 10.0)

Scale	Title	None	Grades 1 – 3	Grades 4 – 6	Grades 7 – 9	Grades 10 – 12	Prob-ability*
57	Social Distance; Race and Religion	49.8	51.0	52.5	52.1	52.6	< .01
37	Need for Unchanging Structure	49.9	51.2	51.9	52.4	54.0	< .01
38 (sub of 37)	Tradition-al Family Ideology	49.7	50.9	51.3	52.8	53.2	< .01
36	Christian Utopian-ism	48.8	51.1	51.6	50.6	53.2	< .01

(Heavy vertical lines between columns separate groups that are significantly different.)
* See chapter note 2.

Tables 3.13 and 3.14 settle the question raised in Table 3.11 as to whether the rather negative characteristics reported there were associated with 3 years or less of attendance or specifically with grades 7 − 9. Clearly the association is with attendance sometime during grades 7 − 9, which in most cases will be attendance in grades 7 − 8. Schools in The Lutheran Church − Missouri Synod generally do not group grades by elementary, junior, and senior high, but rather by grades 1 − 8 and 9 − 12.

Table 3.14 reaffirms the fact already reported that general level of family education and previous membership in another denomination both tend to be less among those who attended only some part of grades 7 − 9. Horatio Alger Orientation is clearly associated more with those attending only grades 7 − 9 than with any other attendance pattern, including never having attended.

TABLE 3.14

**Characteristics More Likely on the Average to be Associated with
Up to 3-Year Attendance Only During Grades 7 − 9
(Average Standardized Score for LCMS Synod Lay People
= 50.0 With Standard Deviation = 10.0)**

Scale	Title	Grades 7 − 9	None	Grades 1 − 3	Grades 4 − 6	Grades 10 − 12	Prob-ability*
55	Family Level of Education	45.5	48.8	50.7	46.2	49.8	< .0001
10	Prior Large Denominational Membership	48.1	52.1	52.3	50.1	50.8	< .001
69	Horatio Alger Orientation	51.9	47.8	48.4	50.4	48.9	< .01

(Heavy vertical lines between columns separate groups that are significantly different.)
* See chapter note 2.

Is there a best time to attend parochial school? If you must attend less than 12 years, it may be better to attend grades 7 − 12. But the benefits are likely to be mixed. In number, the positive and negative characteristics more likely to be associated with those who attended only some part of grades 7 − 9 and those who attended grades 10 − 12 was roughly fifty-fifty (four-to-four and five-to-four). Attendance during no interval of three grades was clearly and indisputably better than any other except that no differences at all were associated with grades 1 – 3. Therefore, as far as the goals of Christian education are concerned, "If you are going to attend parochial school, better attend all 12 grades – or more."

CHAPTER FOUR

Conclusions and Implications

Answers to the 13 Questions

Data from *A Study of Generations* were reorganized for this research. As such they were relatively "neutral" data in that they were not collected with the thought of comparing those who received some or all of their education in the first twelve grades at parochial schools with those who did not.

Nevertheless, the data as summarized and presented in the preceding chapters were addressed to the 13 questions raised in Chapter 1, but the findings were not discussed directly in terms of those 13 questions. Here are the 13 questions with summary answers.

1. *Are those who attended parochial schools different in any way (whether or not that difference can be traced to their parochial education)?* Indeed they are! On the average, those who attended parochial schools for varying lengths of time, and particularly those who attended the longest, differed from those who never attended parochial schools in the ways indicated in Table 4.1.

TABLE 4.1

Ways in Which Those Who Attended Parochial Schools Tended on the Average to Differ Significantly from Those LCMS Members Who Did Not (Clergy and Laity Combined)

Scale	**Much More**	Scale	**More**	Scale	**Slightly More**
8	Biblical Knowledge (belief)	19	Religious Experience (belief)	14	Personal Caring God (belief)
41	Personal Piety (behavior)	58	Awareness of the Immanent Trinity (belief)	66	Emotional Certainty of Faith (belief)
40	Congregational Activity (behavior)	5	Humanity of Jesus (belief)	44	Fundamentalism-Liberalism (belief)

6 Divinity of Jesus
(belief)

16 * Exclusive Truth
Claim of Chris-
tianity (possibly
exaggerated) (belief)

42 Role of the Pastor in
Social Issues (attitude
and opinion)

61 Image of Lutherans as
Different (attitude and
opinion)

28 Transcendental
Meaning in Life
(value)

71 Positive Attitude
Toward Life and
Death (attitude and
opinion)

60 Individual Christian
Responsibility (atti-
tude and opinion)

63 * Peer Orientation
(attitude and
opinion)

51 Acceptance of
Authority (attitude
and opinion)

12 Church, Me, and
Social Justice
(behavior)

21 Personal Evange-
lism (behavior)

47 – 48 Personal Involve-
ment in Church and
Community
(behavior)

74 Personal Initiative
in Church and
Public Issues
(behavior)

70 Gospel Orientation
to Life (behavior)

55 Family Education
Level

Much Less

10 Prior Denominational
Membership
(circumstantial)

Less

15 Salvation by Works
(belief)

Slightly Less

29 Self-development
(value)

9 Biblical Ignorance
(belief)

36 Christian Utopianism
(attitude and opinion)

54 Desire for Detach-
ment from the
World (value)

52 Desire for a
Dependable World

69 Horatio Alger Orienta-
tion (attitude and
opinion)

111

(value)

37 – 38 Need for Unchanging Structure (attitude and opinion)	57 Social Distance; Race and Religion (attitude and opinion)
43 Need for Religious Absolutism (attitude and opinion)	62 Service Without Proclamation (attitude and opinion)
32 – 34 Generalized Prejudice (attitude and opinion)	27 Disappointment with the Church (attitude and opinion)
56 Social Distance; Radical Life Styles (attitude and opinion)	
67 Self-oriented Utilitarianism (attitude and opinion)	
64 Power Orientation to Social Issues (attitude and opinion)	

* Possibly undesirable

These are the ways in which the parochially educated tend to differ from other members, but whether or not any of these differences are due to their parochial school attendance is quite another question.

In a search of the entire *Study of Generations* data bank, the parochially educated were found to have three other characteristics that were more common among them than among other LCMS members: age, eventual level of education attained, and eventually becoming a clergyman. All three of these variables were significantly correlated with length of parochial school attendance.

Therefore, the characteristic differences between the parochially educated and those who never attended were likely due to a variety of reasons including parochial school attendance, age, eventual educational attainment, and later training and experience as pastors.

However, when all the differences due to age, education, and clergy training had been identified, many significant differences were still found to be associated with parochial school attendance. On the basis of the data available in the *Study of Genera-*

tions data bank, the most plausible explanation for the remaining differences is parochial school attendance.

However, this analysis by the process of elimination does not prove that parochial school was the cause. The evidence is necessary but not sufficient. It only raises the probability that parochial school attendance is the cause of the differences still associated with it when age, education, and clergy training had been controlled. We were not able to disprove parochial school attendance as the cause by showing that all of the differences were due to other events or characteristics. Therefore, it would be best to call the remaining differences still associated with length of parochial school attendance "apparent effects" of parochial school attendance or differences "possibly causes" by attending parochial schools during part or all of grades 1 – 12.

The differences possibly caused by parochial school attendance are as follows:

TABLE 4.2

**Differences Associated on the Average with
Parochial School Attendance When Controlled for
Age, Ultimate Education Attained, and Pastoral Training Experience**

Scale	**Much More**	Scale	**More**	Scale	**Slightly More**
19	Religious Experience (belief)	21	Personal Evangelism (behavior)	44	Fundamentalism-Liberalism (belief)
5	Divinity of Jesus (belief)			58	Awareness of the Immanent Trinity (belief)
16 *	Exclusive Truth Claim of Christianity (possibly exaggerated) (belief)			28	Transcendental Meaning in Life (value)
8	Biblical Knowledge (belief)			52 *	Desire for a Dependable World (value)
41	Practices of Personal Piety (behavior)			37 *	Need for Unchanging Structures (attitude and opinion)
				51	Acceptance of Authority (attitude and opinion)
				70	Gospel Oriented Life (behavior)
	Much Less		**Less**		**Slightly Less**
10	Prior Denominational Membership (circumstantial)	15	Salvation by Works (belief)	9	Biblical Ignorance (belief)

	65 * Church Involvement in Social Issues (attitude and opinion)	66 Anxiety Over One's Faith (attitude and opinion)
		64 Power Orientation to Social Issues (attitude and opinion)
		63 Peer Orientation (attitude and opinion)
* Possibly undesirable		

2. *Does longer parochial school attendance produce greater effects?* Yes, very consistently so. Length of parochial school attendance on the average is definitely correlated with magnitude of the differences. Analyses both in terms of length of attendance and most popular patterns of attendance support this conclusion.

The obvious implication is, "If you're going to do it at all, go all the way." If you're going to attend parochial school at all, attend all 12 grades or more for the maximum impact (again assuming that the differences associated with parochial school attendance have probably been caused by that attendance).

Another obvious conclusion is that the old maxim "Give me a child through the age of nine, and I'll leave my mark for life," does not necessarily hold for parochial education. It will not necessarily hold, for that matter, for age 14, which is commonly the time of confirmation and often viewed as an adequate stopping point for parochial education. The longer the attendance, through age 18 at least, the greater the difference, is the general rule through *A Study of Generations* data.

3. *Do certain grades have greater or particularly different impact than others? Or are there certain stages in life when children are apparently more impressionable and thus particularly affected by a parochial education?* No, there is clearly no "best time to attend"; and, if no more than three grades are attended, grades 1 – 3 only or grades 7 – 9 only are clearly not the best times to attend.

When those who attended only various groupings of three

114

grades were compared with each other and with those that never attended, on the average:

a. Those who attended only grades 1 – 3 were in no way different from those who never attended.

b. Those who attended only grades 4 – 6 tended to be significantly different from those who never attended or attended only grades 1 – 3, only in terms of three out of 78 measures (and one of those differences, a greater desire to be socially distant from people of different races and religions, was undesirable).

c. Those who attended only grades 7 – 9 tended to be significantly different (from those who never attend) in terms of only eight measures, only half of which were desirable.

d. Those who attended only grades 10 – 12 were found likely to differ significantly from those who never attended in terms of only nine out of 78 measures, and four of the nine were not particularly desirable.

e. All of these differences were residual differences after controlling for age and clergy training and experience.

Other analyses clarified that attendance during grades 1 – 3 when followed by additional attendance was not without its apparent effects. But any apparent effects of attendance for the first three years *alone* could not be detected by these 78 measures which had already been shown to be generally quite sensitive in *A Study of Generations*.

Implication: Is there something special about instruction in the first three grades that obviously needs improvement? For example, is it possible that consistently the less well-trained teachers are assigned to the primary grades? Or might an examination of methods provide a key?

Considerable recent research in religious education as well as in developmental psychology has identified methods as a key variable in relation both to pupil motivation and pupil maturation. Piaget's [1] many decades of work in description and analysis of the development of intelligence in youth has culminated in identification of stages of readiness for certain kinds of teaching and learning. Piaget's findings parallel very closely Kohlberg's [2] research in development of ·moral judgment and particularly Ronald Goldman's [3] investigation of readiness for religion. All of these researches raise serious questions about not only the utility but even the possible negative consequences of certain kinds of story-telling and especially of moralizing in the primary grades.

A further implication: Are there characteristics common to confirmation instruction programs that concentrate at grades 7 – 8 that need careful reexamination? [4] For example, there are minimal and to a considerable degree undesirable characteristics associated with attendance in parochial school only sometime during grades 7 – 9. These raise serious questions. First, what is the advisability of mounting a concentrated effort in Christian education toward the rite of confirmation near the end of grade 8? Second, what are the effects of involving youth in parochial school, who up to that point have never attended and who do not attend after confirmation? The research mentioned above also raises important questions about the relevance of the methods being used in confirmation instruction and parochial education in general at that point in the developmental process of the youth. The research indicated above supports the contention that inability to handle high level abstractions is characteristic of the majority of young people of average ability at grades 7 – 8. For most of them such ability is not fully developed. At least they are unable to cope well with the highly abstract, logically structured, and doctrinal instruction typical of a religious education and confirmation instruction given at that age. The research indicated that an expected outcome of such instruction is a kind of learning that fixes immature, concrete, and rigid conceptualization that is highly resistant to later influences and developments necessary for the maturing of an articulate adult faith.

Fägerlind's [5] research regarding the teaching of Christianity in public school grades 2, 4, and 6 in Sweden also supports the importance of careful examination of methods at all grade levels. He found that traditional classroom teaching where the greatest part of the time was devoted to the teacher's oral presentation was correlated with declining interest in religion and declining belief over the grades. Use of visual aids and group projects by interested, believing teachers correlated with highest pupil interest. And contrary to what was hypothesized, telling of Bible stories in the lower grades, repetition of familiar Bible stories, and cyclic study of earlier investigated Biblical events in concentric structured curriculum was more interesting to most students. Difficulty in understanding more abstract concepts in upper elementary grades was cited by 20% as the reason they found religion classes boring.

Conversation on ethical and religious subjects in lower grades proved both difficult for teachers and less interesting for pupils. The same held true for Psalms and Prophets for sixth graders while stories about mankind's earliest times and about Jesus' proclamation were generally found interesting.

4. *Have they been affected very much differently by differences in parochial schools over the past 60 years?* Not that it can be demonstrated by these data. Despite popular opinions to the contrary, we found no evidence that parochial schools were particularly better or worse in any past era. The differences associated with parochial education occurred regardless of when those parochial schools were attended between 1910 and 1970.

The new Mission:Life Curriculum represents a major shift that hopefully will produce different graduates than in the past. But since Mission:Life did not become a reality in curriculum until 1970, only future research can tell of its impact.

All of this is not to say that individual schools may not be different, both in curriculum and consequence. But when taken as a whole—all schools and all pupils—elementary and secondary parochial education seems to have had pretty much the same effects on each generation since 1910. At least this is characteristic on the average for those who attended at various times over the last 60 years.

5. *Are they better Lutherans?* Yes, quite definitely so. This is true particularly in terms of Biblical knowledge, doctrinal understanding and assent, personal commitment, certain aspects of congregational activity and leadership, and some evidences of orientation to Gospel rather than Law.

How well do these compare with the objectives of parochial schools? The following is a comprehensive statement of LCMS objectives of Christian education. What is most likely to occur as a consequence of attending parochial schools has been underlined.

> The objective of the Christian education program is that through the Word and Spirit of God, the individual may *know God, especially his seeking and forgiving love in Christ, respond in faith,* and grow up into Christian maturity; and that as the individual sees himself a reconciled, redeemed child of God and a member of Christ's body, the church, he may live happily in peace with God, himself, and his fellowmen, and may express his joy in *worship of God* and in loving service to others; and that in love of God he may value all of God's creative work in his world and church and may *participate actively in God's mission to the church and the world and live in the Christian hope.*[6]

Whether or not greater fulfillment of the objectives underlined above is worth continued long-term support of the schools with teachers, curriculum, money, and long-term attendance, the church must decide. Notice, however, that the activities and attributes underlined above are more characteristic of the parochially educated than of any and all other LCMS members whatever their other Christian education experiences. Many of the non-parochially educated, some of whom had little or no other formal Christian

118

education, participated fully in all other parish education activities.

It is also noteworthy that a much higher proportion of those who attend parochial elementary and secondary schools become clergymen. Whether in this latter case attending parochial school is cause or effect can surely be argued. But the fact still remains: a much higher proportion of those who attend parochial schools eventually become clergy.

6. *Are they more actively (not deeply) involved in church and community life?* We found that generally speaking those who are more actively involved in congregational life are also more active in the community. As a whole, those who attended parochial schools are more actively involved in church and community life. But laity alone generally are not. They are rather more actively engaged in practices of personal piety which include only some phases of congregational life. These phases include the following:

a. Attempting to cooperate with the pastor in his program for the congregation;
b. Feeling they fit well with the groups of people who make up the congregation;
c. Generously giving a higher proportion of their income to church work;
d. Influencing the decisions of the congregation;
e. Talking particularly with members of their own family about Christianity and church,
f. Reading the Bible and Christian literature and spending time in private meditation more regularly, and
g. Consistently trying to put their religion into practice in daily life.

In fact rather than keeping something of a balance between participation in church and community life, if ever confronted with a conflict between the two, they report a greater tendency to participate in church activities. And possibly to the detriment of community life, they are *less* inclined than those who never attended parochial schools to encourage and support the church's involvement in social issues.

7. *Are they then less prejudiced and more humane?* No, they are not. They are about as prejudiced and humane as LCMS members in general, with two exceptions. On the one hand, they are more inclined to favor strong male supremacy and rigid versions of traditional family roles. On the other, they report much greater involvement in personal evangelism, not only among friends, family, and neighbors, but also among strangers.

8. *Are they helped or hindered in coming to grips with the world outside?* There is no strong evidence in either direction. All that can be said about this question can only be said by implication. One could argue that a person who is more fully aware of the grace of God in Jesus Christ, who is more apt to reject any claims of salvation by good works, and who is more inclined to trust salvation to Jesus Christ, is therefore better equipped to face life in all of its dimensions. Yet, these data show no such evidence. The parochially educated are apparently no better adjusted in their occupations. They are no more or less emotionally balanced or inclined toward mental illness, nor are they more or less happy in their family lives. And they are about as involved as their nonparochially educated counterparts in the conflicts and confrontations of private and public life. About the same proportion of them report serious personal or family difficulties during the last year and report seeing counselors of psychotherapists. Unless one wants to argue that their slightly greater desire for a dependable world and need for unchanging structures, particularly in family life, is in and of itself evidence of less effective engagement with the world, one would have to conclude that attendance at parochial schools neither helps nor particularly hinders realistic facing of life.

9. *Do they know more about the Bible?* Definitely so. However, the measures of Biblical knowledge and ignorance or error were so rudimentary that their greater Biblical knowledge appears only to be the difference between practically none and some slight amount. Their degree of Biblical knowledge could be substantial without it being identified by these measures. This is an area that should be researched much more carefully with much more sophisticated measuring instruments than the two regarding Biblical knowledge from *A Study of Generations.* Nevertheless, the fact remains: the parochially educated are more Biblically literate.

10. *Do they have greater tendencies for either legalism or freedom in the Gospel?* Frankly, both! They have a substantially greater tendency toward freedom in the Gospel. At the same time, they have some ambivalent tendencies toward legalism. In terms of orientation toward Law and Gospel, four basic types of believers were identified in analyses following the publication of *A Study of Generations.* These were high Gospel – low Law, high Law – low Gospel, low Law – low Gospel, and high Gospel – high Law. The parochially educated will on the average tend most characteristically to resemble the last of these four types. The typical LCMS member educated in parochial schools during elementary and high school years will tend to be highly oriented to the Gospel and somewhat highly inclined toward the Law (Law is used here in the theological sense in contrast to the Gospel). In other words, though they have found and experienced a great deal of the freeing power of the Gospel, their Christian lives are nevertheless overlayed with a slight legalism. Some so emphasize the exclusive truth claim of Christianity, that there is salvation only in Jesus Christ, that they begin to claim that salvation and truth are to be found only in their particular branch of Christendom, or their synod, or even their congregation. Some are particularly desirous of a very dependable, unchanging world and have begun to equate the structures of

121

society with the givens of God's creation. Some are particularly concerned about what they believe to be the necessity of maintaining male supremacy and authority in all things. Theirs is more than an emphasis on the importance of the husband being the head of the wife and also loving his wife as Christ loved the church and gave Himself for it. Theirs is also a need for a kind of authoritarianism and rigid rules and structures in family life, including need for children to conform and obey with no questions asked, no reasons given.

As a whole, the tendency toward legalism is not as strong as the experience and expression of the Gospel. Nevertheless, a tinge of rigidity and legalism is unquestionably present.

One of the clear implications for educators from *A Study of Generations* applies here:

> . . . one of the two most significant implications for educators (together with a Law-Gospel distinction) is the importance of keeping two emphases in education in balance: (A) learning to *experience* and *express* belonging, mutuality, caring, and relating with people; and (B) learning to *know* the Bible, church history, and doctrine—the content of the faith. Overemphasis on (A) may lead to a tendency toward belief in salvation by works. Overemphasis on (B) may lead to, or be accompanied by, rigidity, authoritarianism, inhumanity, and emphasis on conformity.[7]

It appears that LCMS parochial schools have not kept these two emphases in good balance. Rather, there has probably been too great an emphasis on learning to know. No less learning to know, but more experiences of mutuality and training in the skills of caring about and for other people seem to be in order as an integral part of parochial school curriculum and residential school life.

11. *Do they report more frequent acts of personal service toward others or behaviors that may be described as weaknesses of the flesh?* As a whole, the parochially educated

report more frequent acts of personal service to others and less frequent behaviors that may be described as weaknesses of the flesh. But this is not the case for lay people alone, with one exception—greater practice of personal evangelism. Otherwise, when the effects of age, ultimate level of education achieved, and later training and experiences as clergy are removed, parochial school attendance is associated with no more or less frequent reports of either personal service or questionable (or clearly sinful) personal activities.

12. *Do they report greater or less satisfaction with family life and stability of family life?* Our evidence does not show that the family life of those who attended parochial schools was any more or less satisfactory or stable.

13. *Do they sense greater meaning and purpose of their lives?* It is clear that the parochially educated find meaning in life beyond the physical, material world that they can see and touch. They tend more characteristically to find their meaning in relationships with God and with other people and transcendental values such as forgiveness, eternal life, love, family happiness, and religion as a whole rather than personal values such as power, prestige, adventure, money beauty, and personal achievement. Nevertheless, when asked whether or not they saw meaning and purpose in their lives and experienced particular satisfaction in what they were doing day by day, they evidenced no more or less general sense of meaning and purpose in their lives than others. Apparently any difference in their experience of the significance of their lives is not in degree but in kind.

A Question of Depth

The beliefs of those who attended parochial schools are decidedly different. But as far as changed attitudes and different behaviors are concerned, parochial schools demonstrate little impact other than upon worship attendance and certain practices of personal piety. Cognitive impact seems to be the greatest, affective less, and behavioral the least. If we assume that the differences associated with attending parochial schools are in fact most probably due to that attendance, this summary finding raises questions about the depth of the impact. Beliefs are clearly affected, attitudes less so, behaviors very little.

Is this an artifact of our measuring instruments? Were our measures of beliefs the most sensitive and reliable, measures of attitudes less so, and our measures of behavior rather weak and insensitive? Not at all. Scales measuring reported behavior such as supporting others in crises, personal evangelism, neighborliness, questionable personal activities, congregational activity, personal piety, and personal involvement in church and community were among those with the highest reliabilities (.80 to .90). Measures of attitudes such as generalized prejudice (.86), antisemitism (.84), the role of pastors in social action (.89), and need for unchanging structure (.78) were nearly as strong. And our other studies of characteristic differences of various subgroups showed measures of behavior and attitude to be equally as sensitive as our measures of beliefs. No, this finding of cognitive impact greatest, affective less, and behavioral least is not a reflection of limitations of our measuring instruments but apparently of the impact of the first 12 years of parochial school.

This is a typical result of educational endeavors; but is "typical" all that's possible—even from the same investments? Might the same amount of investment but with different emphases produce better results? Is it possible that parochial schools have been so concerned about meeting secular standards or being up to the level of public schools that they have not emphasized the uniqueness of the Gospel either in curriculum content or in the ways in which schools are administered and run?

Greater concentration on affective teaching-learning without sacrificing the cognitive is clearly implied. For example, are teachers and pupils *experiencing* the love and forgiveness of the Gospel from one another and from parish members and administrators as fully as they are learning *about* it? Are skills of living out the Gospel with one another being modeled and practiced as much as doctrine and challenge to mission are being presented and discussed? Questions such as these get back to learning theory and what educators believe about man. Many emphasize the flow from beliefs to attitudes to behaviors when they theorize about learning, as if the relationship between beliefs and behaviors were a one-way street. It may be that because of the emphasis upon faith in Lutheran theology, this theory of learning has received implicit, if not explicit, encouragement in parochial education. Much learning theory growing out of research in social psychology emphasizes the sequence of structure to process to attitude. Place a person in a new structure of roles and relationships, involve him in new and different processes of behavior, and his attitudes will be found to change over time. Performance of new behaviors has been shown to modify attitudes and beliefs as effectively as change in beliefs apparently affects behaviors.[8] The sequence can well be a two-way street; beliefs through attitudes to behaviors, or behaviors to attitudes to beliefs. Skills training in being the light of the Gospel to other people may well be a helpful and efficient, if not essential, supplement to the teaching-learning of knowledge, understanding, and acceptance of doctrine and dogma.

Specifics for Special Consideration

Both Tables 4.1 and 4.2 show that the effects most likely due to parochial school attendance are for the most part considerable and positive. They include:

1. More frequent reporting of personal experiences with God;
2. More consistent belief in the divinity of Jesus;
3. Greater clarity on the way of salvation by grace through faith in Jesus Christ alone;
4. Clearly more Biblical knowledge;
5. A much fuller devotional life and witnessing to others about Jesus and His church;

125

6. Balanced conservation doctrine (neither liberal nor ultraconservative);
7. A greater awareness of the presence of the Trinity in one's whole life;
8. Highest value given to relationships with God and men;
9. Reasonable respect for authority;
10. Strong tendencies to be forgiving and personally forthright with other people, at the same time that there are definite tendencies to reject belief in salvation by works;
11. Avoidance of oversimplistic views of social issues merely as power struggles; and
12. Less tendency to be anxious about one's faith or to be overly swayed by one's peers.

Though the general picture concerning parochial education's effects is wholesome and healthy, there is still room for improvement. A number of specifics need special consideration in the curriculum and administration of parochial schools.

1. Attendance does not have divisive effects, but neither does it decrease desire to remain socially distant from many disadvantaged and less fortunate groups and individuals, nor does it reduce prejudice.
2. There is no evidence of increased social concern growing out of parochial school attendance although there are some strong hints of increased resistance to the church's involvement in social issues.
3. The parochially educated are no more involved in community leadership or personal service to other individuals than are other church members.
4. There is no evidence of clearer sense of life purpose.
5. Proportion of illnesses, both physical and emotional, is no different.
6. There is only slight evidence of less legalism and suffering under the burden of the Law (rather than the freedom of the Gospel) among the parochially educated.
7. Parochial education is associated with greater need for both stable and somewhat authoritarian family structures.

There will obviously be differences of opinion as to the appropriateness of expecting many of these things to result from attending parochial schools. But to the degree that any of these specifics are appropriate expectations, they deserve the reconsideration, study, ingenuity, and special effort of administrators, teachers, pastors, parents, and students.

Need for Further Research

This research has demonstrated that it is highly probable that parochial education is not without results but is not likely productive of both definite and good effects. From time to time throughout this report, references have been made to needs for additional research to pursue certain questions or clarify ambiguous findings. In addition, there are two major kinds of research needed to maximally advise parochial education. First, carefully designed and executed field experiments in which randomly selected schools, teachers, and pupils are randomly assigned a variety of teaching-learning experiences in which methods of teaching-learning are contrasted and their differential effects are investigated by highly sophisticated statistical analyses. Second, researches in which the differential effects of a given curriculum are investigated for pupils from homes of contrasting religious environments where much more than superficial indicators such as church attendance, monetary contribution, and frequency of family devotions are used to identify those religious environments.

Appendix A

The 33 chi-square tables presented in this appendix are discussed in the last section of Chapter 2.

Some response categories for a few items have been combined. For some items the original five categories of length of attendance have been combined into four. Categories were combined in these two fashions in order to meet the requirements for valid Chi-square tests that (1) no *expected* frequencies be less than one, and (2) no more than 20% of the *expected* frequencies for any table be five or less.

The *observed* frequencies reported in each table are for the total sample (both lay people and clergy) minus nonrespondents for the particular item.

Item 135: (Mark the number of organizations of each kind to which you belong, or for which you are an advisor, counselor, sponsor, etc.):

SCHOOL SERVICE GROUPS, such as PTA, or alumni associations, Y-Teens, Hi-Y

Number of Organizations Years Attended Parochial	0	1	2-4
None	661	219	53
1 – 3 yrs.	255	51	12
4 – 6 yrs.	47	22	4
7 – 9 yrs.	81	34	11
10 – 12 yrs.	23	16	5

$$X^2 = 26.14 \qquad df = 8 \qquad p = .001$$

Item 142: (Mark the number of organizations of each kind to which you belong, or for which you are an advisor, counselor, sponsor, etc.):

INDEPENDENT VOLUNTARY RELIGIOUS ORGANIZATIONS, such as Lutheran Evangelistic Movement, YMCA, YWCA, Lutheran Medical Mission Association, World Brotherhood Exchange

Number of Organizations / Years Attended Parochial	0	1	2-4
None	841	77	11
1 – 3 yrs.	283	24	11
4 – 6 yrs.	59	12	2
7 – 9 yrs.	139	26	5
10 – 12 yrs.			

$X^2 = 2.73$ df = 6   p = .001

Item 190: How important to you is SOCIAL JUSTICE (fair treatment of all)?

Response Possibilities / Years Attended Parochial	Extreme Import.	Quite Import.	Some Import.	Least Import.
None	132	232	309	216
1 – 3 yrs.	42	79	109	64
4 – 6 yrs.	8	18	26	18
7 – 9 yrs.	23	27	46	27
10 – 12 yrs.	1	16	14	11

$X^2 = 11.01$ df = 12   p = .53

Item 197: Mark the number of close friends (not family or relatives) you have, people whom you feel really care about you.

Number of Close Friends / Years Attended Parochial	0 – 2	3	4	5	6	7 or more
None	83	76	112	69	65	521
1 – 3 yrs.	32	30	26	18	19	194
4 – 6 yrs.	7	3	9	4	5	44
7 – 12 yrs.	16	9	18	15	17	94

$X^2 = 26.10$ df = 24   p = .04

Item 217: Are you frequently ill?

Response Possibilities Years Attended Parochial	Yes	No
None	52	860
1 – 3 yrs.	19	285
4 – 6 yrs.	6	66
7 – 9 yrs.	5	118
10 – 12 yrs.	1	41

$$X^2 = 2.57 \qquad df = 4$$
$$p = .63$$

Item 218: Have you had serious difficulties in your home (prolonged illness, unemployment, death, or injuries, personal problems) during the past year?

Response Possibilities Years Attended Parochial	Yes	No
None	204	706
1 – 3 yrs.	68	234
4 – 6 yrs.	14	58
7 – 9 yrs.	30	93
10 – 12 yrs.	5	37

$$X^2 = 3.28 \qquad df = 4$$
$$p = .51$$

Item 219: Have you ever gone to a psychologist, psychiatrist, or some other therapist for help with your emotional problems?

Response Possibilities Years Attended Parochial	Yes	No
None	64	845
1 – 3 yrs.	22	277
4 – 6 yrs.	6	65
7 – 9 yrs.	11	112
10 – 12 yrs.	1	41

$$X^2 = 2.23 \qquad df = 4$$
$$p = .69$$

Item 220: Are you or someone in your immediate family now receiving welfare aid? (Do not include unemployment compensation.)

Response Possibilities Years Attended Parochial	Yes	No
None	36	874
1 – 3 yrs.	10	290
4 – 6 yrs.	2	69
7 – 12 yrs.	6	159

$$X^2 = 2.09 \qquad df = 3$$
$$p = .57$$

130

Item 280: How do you feel about your family life?
   a. I am happy about it.
   b. I am quite happy about it, but I have a few complaints.
   c. There are many things which I do not like about it, but in some ways I am happy with it.
   d. I am not happy about it.
   e. I do not have much feeling one way or the other.
   f. I would rather not say.
   g. This isn't part of my experience at present.

Response Possibilities Years Attended Parochial	A	B	C – D – E	F – G
None	455	359	111	23
1 – 3 yrs.	171	91	47	13
4 – 6 yrs.	35	23	13	3
7 – 12 yrs.	74	68	21	7

$$X^2 = 16.10 \qquad df = 9 \qquad p = .07$$

Item 282: How do you feel about your work?
   (Same response possibilities as Item 280 above)

Response Possibilities Years Attended Parochial	A	B	C	D	E	F – G
None	307	299	125	21	13	155
1 – 3 yrs.	127	100	43	9	5	35
4 – 6 yrs.	25	30	5	1	1	12
7 – 12 yrs.	57	70	17	5	2	19

$$X^2 = 19.76 \qquad df = 15 \qquad p = .17$$

Item 431: Concerns about caution have little place when the issue is one of social injustice.

Response Possibilities Years Attended Parochial	Strongly Agree	Agree	Disagree	Strongly Disagree
None	37	311	530	30
1 – 3 yrs.	15	131	161	8
4 – 6 yrs.	3	21	45	3
7 – 12 yrs.	6	51	106	4

$$X^2 = 10.83 \qquad df = 9 \qquad p = .28$$

Item 451: The church should never be silent over an injustice in a local community.

Response Possibilities Years Attended Parochial	Strongly Agree	Agree	Disagree & Strongly Disagree
None	133	523	264
1 – 3 yrs.	57	174	89
4 – 6	6	50	17
7 – 9 yrs.	17	66	30
10 – 12 yrs.	8	30	6

$X^2 = 12.41$ df = 8   p = .13

Item 478: It doesn't matter so much what I believe as long as I lead a moral life.
  a. I definitely disagree
  b. I tend to disagree
  c. I tend to agree
  d. I definitely agree

Response Possibilities Years Attended Parochial	A	B	C – D
None	507	268	184
1 – 3	181	85	67
4 – 6 yrs.	56	15	7
7 – 12 yrs.	117	41	15

$X^2 = 26.08$ df = 6   p = .0002

Item 480: Although I am a religious person, I refuse to let religious considerations influence my everyday affairs.
  a. Definitely not true of me
  b. Tends not to be true
  c. Tends to be true
  d. Clearly true in my case

Response Possibilities Years Attended Parochial	A	B	C	D
None	330	379	211	32
1 – 3 yrs.	108	118	77	28
4 – 6 yrs.	28	35	10	5
7 – 9 yrs.	52	42	26	8
10 – 12 yrs.	28	11	2	2

$X^2 = 40.60$ df = 12   p = .00006

132

Item 481: If not prevented by unavoidable circumstances, I attend worship services
a. More than once a week
b. About once a week
c. Two or three times a month
d. Less than once a month

Response Possibilities — Years Attended Parochial	A	B	C	D
None	61	540	212	141
1 – 3 yrs.	37	193	64	37
4 – 6 yrs.	13	48	7	9
7 – 9 yrs.	16	83	20	10
10 – 12 yrs.	18	23	2	1

$X^2 = 87.59$ $df = 12$ $p = < .00001$

Item 483: Although I believe in my religion, I feel there are many more important things in my life.

Response Possibilities — Years Attended Parochial	Definitely Disagree	Tend to Disagree	Tend to or Definitely Agree
None	369	348	240
1 – 3 yrs.	152	96	86
4 – 6 yrs.	46	19	13
7 – 9 yrs.	68	36	25
10 – 12 yrs.	31	8	5

$X^2 = 37.39$ $df = 8$ $p = .00001$

Item 485: The only benefit one receives from prayer is psychological.

Response Possibilities — Years Attended Parochial	Definitely Disagree	Tend to Disagree	Tend to Agree & Definitely Agree
None	532	278	143
1 – 3 yrs.	198	74	62
4 – 6 yrs.	49	17	11
7 – 9 yrs.	92	27	10
10 – 12 yrs.	39	4	1

$X^2 = 36.06$ $df = 8$ $p = .00002$

Item 549: During the last year what was the average *monthly* contribution of your family to your local congregation?

Average Monthly Contrib. / Years Attended Parochial	Under $5	$5–$24	$25–$49	$50 & Up	Don't Know
None	116	343	237	195	64
1–3 yrs.	37	114	83	77	23
4–6 yrs.	6	26	16	22	7
7–9 yrs.	10	30	33	41	13
10–12 yrs.	0	6	15	23	0

$$X^2 = 50.58 \qquad df = 16 \qquad p = .00002$$

Item 500: Compared with my *mother* (If you were not raised by your mother, answer for the woman who had most responsibility for you in your childhood.)

Response Possibilities / Years Attended Parochial	I am much more religious	I am somewhat more religious	I am about as religious	I am somewhat less religious	I am much less religious
None	138	177	419	164	58
1–3 yrs.	31	62	185	41	15
4–6 yrs.	9	11	38	17	2
7–9 yrs.	9	15	74	21	7
10–12 yrs.	2	10	32	0	0

$$X^2 = 46.70 \qquad df = 16 \qquad p = .00008$$

Item 551: Compared with my *father* (If you were not raised by your father, answer for the man who had most responsibility for you in your childhood.)

Response Possibilities / Years Attended Parochial	I am much more religious	I am somewhat more religious	I am about as religious	I am somewhat or much less religious
None	251	244	317	131
1–3 yrs.	52	76	149	55
4–6 yrs.	14	15	34	14
7–9 yrs.	18	19	67	23
10–12 yrs.	5	9	25	5

$$X^2 = 51.27 \qquad df = 12 \qquad p = .00001$$

Item 568: Bring a grievance to the attention of the boss.

HR — I have been asked (or have had opportunity) to do this, but *have refused.*

WR — I have never been asked (or had opportunity), but I *would refuse* if asked.

HT — I have done this, but I really did not want to. I felt I *had to* do it.

WD — I have not been asked, but if I were, I *would do* this.

HD — I have been asked, and I *have done* this willingly.

Response Possibilities / Years Attended Parochial	HR	WR	HT	WD	HD
None	49	117	156	379	223
1 – 3 yrs.	30	59	47	114	67
4 – 6 yrs.	4	9	10	34	18
7 – 9 yrs.	4	6	17	63	32
10 – 12 yrs.	0	3	8	26	5

$$X^2 = 41.47 \qquad df = 16 \qquad p = .00047$$

Item 569: Ask for an increase in wages at the job.

(Same response possibilities as Item 568 above)

Response Possibilities / Years Attended Parochial	HR	WR	HT	WD	HD
None	44	157	139	360	199
1 – 3 yrs.	28	53	65	117	48
4 – 6 yrs.	4	8	7	36	17
7 – 9 yrs.	3	16	20	52	24
10 – 12 yrs.	4	7	9	16	5

$$X^2 = 28.86 \qquad df = 16 \qquad p = .02$$

Item 574: Serve as a picket during a strike.

(Same response possibilities as Items 568 and 569 above)

Response Possibilities / Years Attended Parochial	HR	WR	HT	WD	HD
None	40	618	29	196	41
1 – 3 yrs.	23	202	21	46	21
4 – 6 yrs.	6	46	2	17	3
7 – 9 yrs.	3	88	8	21	4
10 – 12 yrs.	1	26	1	10	1

$$X^2 = 26.09 \qquad df = 12 \qquad p = .02$$

135

Item 602: My family seldom does anything about helping meet social problems.

Response Possibilities / Years Attended Parochial	No	Yes
None	654	292
1 – 3 yrs.	239	81
4 – 6 yrs.	56	22
7 – 9 yrs.	91	36
10 – 12 yrs.	35	9

$X^2 = 5.32$ df = 4
p = .26

Item 604: My family would support neighborhood efforts to keep out persons of other races.

Response Possibilities / Years Attended Parochial	No	Yes
None	823	123
1 – 3 yrs.	269	51
4 – 6 yrs.	69	9
7 – 9 yrs.	121	6
10 – 12 yrs.	43	1

$X^2 = 14.93$ df = 4
p = .005

Item 623: What is your experience in church school teaching?

    a. I am presently teaching church school (or taught this last school year).
    b. I have taught church school previously but not this school year.
    c. I have never taught church school.

Response Possibilities / Years Attended Parochial	A	B	C
None	98	214	635
1 – 3 yrs.	46	58	225
4 – 6 yrs.	13	18	46
7 – 9 yrs.	29	24	74
10 – 12 yrs.	25	5	13

$X^2 = 92.76$ df = 8   p = < .00001

Item 624: By comparison with 5 years ago, the percentage of my income I am now giving to *nonchurch* charities is

    a. Greater   b. About the same   c. Less

Response Possibilities / Years Attended Parochial	A	B	C
None	317	465	160
1 – 3 yrs.	99	170	57
4 – 6 yrs.	23	39	13
7 – 9 yrs.	43	68	12
10 – 12 yrs.	23	20	1

$X^2 = 16.81$ df = 8   p = .04

136

Item 628: Listened to a friend's (or neighbor's) problems and tried to give help or advice.

F. Frequently   O. Occasionally   N. Never

Response Possibilities / Years Attended Parochial	F	O	N
None	413	523	23
1 – 3 yrs.	121	193	16
4 – 6 yrs.	39	38	0
7 – 12 yrs.	86	83	3

$X^2 = 17.19$ $df = 6$ $p = .009$

Item 645: Helped a friend catch up with assignments that he had missed.
(Same response possibilities as Item 628 above)

Response Possibilities / Years Attended Parochial	F	O	N
None	68	524	331
1 – 3 yrs.	28	183	108
4 – 6 yrs.	9	44	23
7 – 9 yrs.	7	67	50
10 – 12 yrs.	1	25	18

$X^2 = 6.93$ $df = 8$ $p = .54$

Item 674: Gave old clothing or furniture or other things to a charitable organization (Goodwill, Salvation Army) or a church sponsored secondhand store.

(Same response possibilities as Item 645 above)

Response Possibilities / Years Attended Parochial	F	O	N
None	271	626	59
1 – 3 yrs.	101	216	14
4 – 6 yrs.	18	50	9
7 – 9 yrs.	43	80	4
10 – 12 yrs.	11	33	0

$X^2 = 13.84$ $df = 8$ $p = .09$

137

Item 721: How active was your *father* in church during your youth?
   a. Very active
   b. Moderately active
   c. Hardly active at all
   d. Had nothing to do with church

Response Possibilities / Years Attended Parochial	A	B	C	D
None	162	237	299	248
1 – 3 yrs.	99	111	75	42
4 – 6 yrs.	29	27	16	5
7 – 9 yrs.	53	42	25	9
10 – 12 yrs.	26	8	6	3

$X^2 = 142.76$ df $= 12$ p $= < .000001$

Item 722: How active was your *mother* in church during your youth?
   (Same response possibilities as Item 721 above)

Response Possibilities / Years Attended Parochial	A	B	C	D
None	201	376	284	93
1 – 3 yrs.	111	132	70	16
4 – 6 yrs.	28	30	18	2
7 – 9 yrs.	48	56	21	4
10 – 12 yrs.	17	18	8	1

$X^2 = 59.09$ df $= 12$ p $= < .00001$

Item 732: Are you now
   a. Single (never married)
   b. Married once
   c. Divorced and single
   d. Divorced and remarried
   e. Widowed
   f. Widowed and remarried

Response Possibilities / Years Attended Parochial	A	B	C&D	E&F
None	194	658	75	29
1 – 3 yrs.	78	211	24	12
4 – 12 yrs.	70	166	12	3

$X^2 = 12.19$ df $= 6$ p $= .06$

138

Appendix B

The design of this study begins with a description of significant differences between members of The Lutheran Church — Missouri Synod who reported no parochial school attendance and those who reported varying numbers of years of attendance from one through 12. In the second step of the design, the effects of age and education, both correlated with parochial school attendance, were controlled to see if the differences associated with attendance were still persistent. In the third step of the analytic design, age, education, and the effect of being a clergyman with all of the additional training and experience that that entails, were simultaneously controlled, again to see if the difference associated with parochial school attendance would still persist.

The tables that follow summarize the three steps for each of the scales that at one of the three stages of the design shows significant differences between the parochially educated and those who never attended. Scales omitted from this appendix showed no significant differences at any of the three stages of the analysis.

Scores shown in the tables were standardized for lay people of The Lutheran Church — Missouri Synod with the average (mean) equal to 50.0 and the standard deviation equal to 10.0.

The column headed "Probability" lists the probability that sample differences as large as those shown in the corresponding row occurred by chance alone rather than due to some systematic cause.

The column headed "Diff." lists the difference between the highest and the lowest subgroup-average-score for the corresponding row. Negative difference scores indicate that the average scores for subgroups decreased with number of years of attendance. Positive difference scores indicate that average subgroup scores increased with increase of number of years of attendance, generally speaking.

Though the question about length of parochial school attendance originally allowed respondents to indicate one of five categories of attendance (none, 1−3 years, 4−6 years, 7−9 years, and 10−12 years), during the last two stages of the analyses it was necessary to combine the five attendance categories into three as they appear in the tables that follow. This condensation of the data was required in order that there might be adequate numbers of persons in each cell of the three-way analyses of variance.

	Length of Parochial School Attendance				
	None	1 – 6 years	7 – 12 years	Prob-ability	Diff.
Scale 5, Humanity of Jesus					
Description (All Respondents)	50.8	50.2	54.0	< .0001	3.2
Controlled by Age and Education	50.8	50.7	53.6	.02	2.9
Controlled by Age, Education, and Clergy Training	50.4	48.9	49.2	.02	−1.5
Scale 6, Divinity of Jesus					
Description (All Respondents)	48.9	51.7	54.6	< .0001	5.7
Controlled by Age and Education	49.2	53.4	54.6	< .00001	5.4
Controlled by Age, Education, and Clergy Training	49.0	52.3	54.3	< .00001	5.3
Scale 8, Biblical Knowledge					
Description (All Respondents)	49.9	50.9	56.5	< .00001	6.6
Controlled by Age and Education	49.8	50.8	56.5	< .00001	6.7
Controlled by Age, Education, and Clergy Training	49.3	49.3	55.0	< .00001	5.7
Scale 9, Biblical Ignorance					
Description (All Respondents)	50.0	49.4	45.8	< .0001	−4.2
Controlled by Age and Education	50.0	49.1	45.8	< .0001	−4.2
Controlled by Age, Education, and Clergy Training	50.9	49.7	47.1	< .01	−3.8
Scale 10, Prior Denominational Membership (Larger Church Bodies)					
Description (All Respondents)	51.9	48.0	46.0	< .00001	−5.9
Controlled by Age and Education	51.9	48.3	45.8	< .00001	−6.1
Controlled by Age, Education, and Clergy Training	52.1	49.3	46.2	< .00001	−5.9
Scale 12, The Church, Me, and Social Justice					
Description (All Respondents)	50.0	50.8	53.1	< .001	3.1
Controlled by Age and Education	49.8	50.6	52.9	< .01	3.1
Controlled by Age, Education, and Clergy Training	49.5	49.8	51.5	< .15	2.0
Scale 14, A Personal, Caring God					
Description (All Respondents)	49.9	50.5	52.6	< .01	2.7
Controlled by Age and Education	50.0	51.0	52.4	.03	2.4
Controlled by Age, Education, and Clergy Training	49.9	50.9	52.3	.02	2.4
Scale 15, Salvation by Works					
Description (All Respondents)	49.7	49.6	43.3	< .0001	−6.4
Controlled by Age and Education	49.6	48.8	43.4	< .00001	−6.2
Controlled by Age, Education, and Clergy Training	50.0	50.1	45.8	< .0001	−4.3

Scale 16, The Exclusive Truth Claim of Christianity Exaggerated

Description (All Respondents)	49.0	52.3	52.8	< .0001	3.8
Controlled by Age and Education		Interaction		< .01	
Controlled by Age, Education, and Clergy Training	48.5	51.4	53.0	< .00001	4.5

Scale 19, Religious Experience

Description (All Respondents)	48.9	52.5	52.6	< .0001	3.7
Controlled by Age and Education	46.5	50.1	50.4	< .00001	3.9
Controlled by Age, Education, and Clergy Training	48.7	52.2	52.4	< .00001	3.7

Scale 21, Personal Evangelism

Description (All Respondents)	49.9	53.2	57.1	< .0001	7.2
Controlled by Age and Education	49.4	53.5	57.7	< .00001	8.3
Controlled by Age, Education, and Clergy Training	48.7	51.0	52.3	< .0001	3.6

Scale 27, Disappointment with the Church

Description (All Respondents)	49.6	50.7	47.6	< .001	− 3.1
Controlled by Age and Education	49.6	50.0	47.5	.06	− 2.5
Controlled by Age, Education, and Clergy Training	49.8	50.2	48.9	.49	− 1.3

Scale 28, Transcendental Meaning in Life

Description (All Respondents)	49.5	51.0	52.9	< .0001	3.4
Controlled by Age and Education	49.6	50.9	52.9	< .0001	3.3
Controlled by Age and Education, and Clergy Training	49.3	50.9	52.0	< .01	2.7

Scale 29, Values of Self-Development

Description (All Respondents)	49.5	50.3	47.8	< .01	− 2.5
Controlled by Age and Education	49.4	49.4	47.8	.07	− 1.6
Controlled by Age, Education, and Clergy Training	49.6	49.9	48.8	.61	− 1.1

Scale 32, Prejudice Toward the Disadvantaged

Description (All Respondents)	49.8	49.4	46.0	< .0001	− 3.8
Controlled by Age and Education	50.0	49.0	46.7	< .001	− 3.3
Controlled by Age, Education, and Clergy Training	50.4	50.4	49.8	.77	− 0.6

Scale 34, Generalized Prejudice

Description (All Respondents)	49.6	49.7	46.1	< .0001	− 3.6
Controlled by Age and Education	49.8	49.3	46.6	< .001	− 3.2
Controlled by Age, Education, and Clergy Training	50.0	50.5	49.3	.48	− 1.2

Scale 36, Christian Utopianism

Description (All Respondents)	49.1	51.4	50.4	< .01	2.3
Controlled by Age and Education	49.0	50.8	49.9	.03	1.8
Controlled by Age, Education, and Clergy Training	48.9	50.8	50.0	.03	1.9

	Length of Parochial School Attendance				
	None	1–6 years	7–12 years	Prob-ability	Diff.
Scale 37, Need for Unchanging Structure					
Description (All Respondents)	49.2	50.7	48.0	< .0001	−2.7
Controlled by Age and Education	49.1	50.0	48.2	.15	−1.8
Controlled by Age, Education, and Clergy Training	49.2	50.1	50.0	.03	−0.9
Scale 38, Need for Unchanging Family Structure					
Description (All Respondents)	48.6	50.1	48.0	< .001	−2.1
Controlled by Age and Education	48.8	50.3	48.6	.07	−1.7
Controlled by Age, Education, and Clergy Training	48.9	51.1	50.4	< .01	−2.2
Scale 40, Congregational Activity					
Description (All Respondents)	49.8	51.9	54.5	< .00001	4.7
Controlled by Age and Education	49.6	52.1	54.0	< .00001	4.4
Controlled by Age, Education, and Clergy Training	49.2	50.8	51.3	.02	2.1
Scale 41, Personal Piety					
Description (All Respondents)	49.7	52.1	56.2	< .00001	6.5
Controlled by Age and Education	49.7	52.3	56.3	< .00001	6.6
Controlled by Age, Education, and Clergy Training	49.4	51.3	54.1	< .00001	4.7
Scale 42, The Role of Pastors in Social Action					
Description (All Respondents)	49.9	50.7	51.9	< .01	2.0
Controlled by Age and Education	49.5	50.5	51.5	.05	2.0
Controlled by Age, Education, and Clergy Training	49.0	49.8	49.0	.76	−0.8
Scale 43, Need for Religious Absolutism					
Description (All Respondents)	49.5	50.4	47.6	< .001	−2.8
Controlled by Age and Education	49.4	49.6	48.1	.23	−1.5
Controlled by Age, Education, and Clergy Training	49.6	50.5	49.2	.40	−1.3
Scale 44, Fundamentalism-Liberalism					
Description (All Respondents)	49.4	50.9	52.0	< .01	2.6
Controlled by Age and Education	49.7	50.7	52.1	.01	2.4
Controlled by Age, Education, and Clergy Training	49.4	50.6	52.4	< .01	3.0
Scale 47, Personal Involvement in Church and Community					
Description (All Respondents)	50.6	50.4	55.3	< .0001	4.9
Controlled by Age and Education	50.6	50.9	55.1	< .0001	4.5
Controlled by Age, Education, and Clergy Training	50.1	49.4	52.6	.02	3.2

142

Scale 48, Personal Involvement in Church

Description (All Respondents)	50.5	50.6	55.3	< .0001	4.8
Controlled by Age and Education	50.5	50.9	55.1	< .00001	4.6
Controlled by Age, Education, and Clergy Training	50.0	49.5	52.8	.02	3.3

Scale 51, Acceptance of Authority

Description (All Respondents)	50.8	48.8	51.9	< .001	3.1
Controlled by Age and Education	49.8	49.2	52.0	.01	2.8
Controlled by Age, Education, and Clergy Training	50.6	48.6	51.7	< .01	3.1

Scale 52, Desire for a Dependable World

Description (All Respondents)	49.2	51.4	48.5	< .001	−2.9
Controlled by Age and Education	48.8	50.6	48.7	.03	−1.9
Controlled by Age, Education, and Clergy Training	48.8	51.0	49.1	.01	−2.2

Scale 54, Desire for Detachment from the World

Description (All Respondents)	49.2	50.9	48.7	< .001	−2.2
Controlled by Age and Education	49.0	49.8	48.8	.43	−1.0
Controlled by Age, Education, and Clergy Training	49.2	50.6	49.2	.21	−1.4

Scale 55, Family Level of Education

Description (All Respondents)	51.2	49.6	54.2	< .0001	4.6
Controlled by Age and Education		Interaction		< .00001	
Controlled by Age, Education, and Clergy Training	50.5	50.5	50.8	.55	0.3

Scale 56, Social Distance — Radical Life Styles

Description (All Respondents)	49.4	49.7	46.2	< .001	−3.5
Controlled by Age and Education	49.9	49.7	47.1	< .01	−2.8
Controlled by Age, Education, and Clergy Training	50.1	51.0	50.0	.42	−1.0

Scale 57, Social Distance — Racial and Religious Groups

Description (All Respondents)	49.0	51.0	48.6	< .01	−2.4
Controlled by Age and Education	50.5	52.1	50.4	.15	−1.7
Controlled by Age, Education, and Clergy Training	49.3	50.7	49.5	.11	−1.4

Scale 58, Awareness of the Immanent Trinity

Description (All Respondents)	50.0	50.6	54.1	< .0001	4.1
Controlled by Age and Education	50.3	51.4	54.2	< .0001	3.9
Controlled by Age, Education, and Clergy Training	50.0	50.9	53.3	< .01	3.3

Scale 60, Individual Christian Responsibility

Description (All Respondents)	50.2	50.4	53.1	< .001	2.9
Controlled by Age and Education	50.0	50.4	52.6	.03	2.6

143

| | Length of Parochial School Attendance | | | | |
	None	1–6 years	7–12 years	Prob-ability	Diff.
Controlled by Age, Education, and Clergy Training	49.8	49.6	51.6	.18	2.0
Scale 61, Image of Lutherans as Different					
Description (All Respondents)	49.7	50.3	52.7	< .01	3.0
Controlled by Age and Education	49.5	49.8	52.2	.02	2.7
Controlled by Age, Education, and Clergy Training	49.3	49.7	52.0	.03	2.7
Scale 62, Service Without Proclamation					
Description (All Respondents)	49.6	49.8	47.3	< .01	−2.5
Controlled by Age and Education	49.3	48.8	47.4	.08	−1.9
Controlled by Age, Education, and Clergy Training		Interaction		.009	
Scale 63, Peer Orientation					
Description (All Respondents)	49.1	51.7	49.8	< .001	−2.6
Controlled by Age and Education	48.8	51.4	49.5	< .001	−2.6
Controlled by Age, Education, and Clergy Training	48.7	50.9	48.6	< .01	−2.3
Scale 64, Power Orientation to Social Issues					
Description (All Respondents)	49.6	50.7	46.7	< .0001	−4.0
Controlled by Age and Education	49.3	48.9	46.3	< .01	−3.0
Controlled by Age, Education, and Clergy Training	49.4	49.1	46.5	.01	−2.6
Scale 66, Emotional Certainty of Faith					
Description (All Respondents)	50.0	50.3	52.1	< .01	2.1
Controlled by Age and Education	50.3	50.7	52.1	.09	1.8
Controlled by Age, Education, and Clergy Training	50.0	50.3	51.7	.16	1.7
Scale 67, Self-Oriented Utilitarianism					
Description (All Respondents)	49.3	50.7	46.1	< .0001	−4.6
Controlled by Age and Education	49.0	49.4	43.5	< .01	−5.9
Controlled by Age, Education, and Clergy Training	48.4	50.4	48.2	.09	−2.2
Scale 69, Horatio Alger Orientation					
Description (All Respondents)	49.4	51.2	49.0	< .01	−2.2
Controlled by Age and Education	49.8	50.6	49.0	.27	−1.6
Controlled by Age, Education, and Clergy Training	49.6	50.6	49.5	.46	−1.1
Scale 70, Gospel-Oriented Life					
Description (All Respondents)	49.9	50.8	53.7	< .0001	3.8
Controlled by Age and Education	49.7	50.9	54.0	< .0001	4.3

144

Controlled by Age, Education, and Clergy Training	49.6	50.1	52.6	< .01	3.0

**Scale 71, Attitudes Toward
Life and Death**

Description (All Respondents)	50.0	50.0	52.6	< .001	2.6
Controlled by Age and Education	49.8	50.5	52.5	< .01	2.7
Controlled by Age, Education, and Clergy Training	49.5	50.3	51.9	.06	2.4

**Scale 74, Personal Initiative
on Church and Public Issues**

Description (All Respondents)	51.1	52.4	58.2	< .0001	7.1
Controlled by Age and Education	51.1	54.2	59.1	< .0001	8.0
Controlled by Age, Education, and Clergy Training	50.4	50.0	51.8	.29	1.8

145

Notes

CHAPTER ONE NOTES

1. Greeley, Andrew M. and Rossi, Peter H. *The Education of Catholic Americans*. National Opinion Research Center Monographs in Social Research No. 6. Chicago: Aldine, 1966. p. ix.

2. Johnstone, Ronald L. *The Effectiveness of Lutheran Elementary and Secondary Schools as Agencies of Christian Education: An Empirical Evaluation Study of the Impact of Lutheran Parochial Schools on the Beliefs, Attitudes, and Behavior of Lutheran Youth*. St. Louis: Concordia Seminary, 1966. p. 23.

3. The reasoning was as follows: A two-way analysis of variance crossing age with amount of parochial school attendance could have four possible major significant outcomes. One, age alone could prove to be a significant main effect, i. e., age could be found to be an independent source of differences in scores on whatever belief, etc., was being measured. This would mean that regardless of the amount of parochial school attendance a person experienced, his age would independently affect his score. People differ systematically regarding what was being measured depending on how old they are. Two, amount of parochial schooling could prove to be a significant main effect, meaning people differ systematically regarding what was being measured depending on how long they attended parochial schools. Three, both age and amount of parochial schooling could prove to be main effects, meaning that both age and attendance were *independently* affecting the scores people received on the variable being measured. Four, age and amount of parochial schooling could prove to be interacting which would mean that age and attendance were not operating as independent or separate "causes" but were *combining* their effects in an unusual way that could not be predicted on the basis of the independent or separate impact of each of them. This would be the case if the *same amount* of parochial schooling *at different times* in history produced (was correlated with) *different* effects (different scores on the variable being measured).

4. Generally, statistical tests are used for the purpose of answering the question, "What's the probability of getting a difference this large between sample subgroups (for example, between the parochially educated and those educated in other schools), if on the average, in the total population from which the sample is taken, there is no such difference between those subgroups?" When small samples of say 30 or so people are used and only a single hypothesis is being tested, it is conventional to require test results that can be expected less than one in 20 times by chance (probability of .05) or less than once in 100 times by chance (probability of .01) before rejecting the hypothesis of no-difference (the null hypothesis) and concluding that the difference found between the sample subgroups is evidence of a significant difference between subgroups of the whole population under study.

Secondly, as size of sample increases, it is easier and easier to highlight differences between comparison groups that are statistically significant but *practically* trivial. A difference that is statistically significant is not always of practical significance. For example, with a sample as large as in this study differences between subgroups in the sample that could occur once in 20 times by chance could be as small as one-tenth of a standard deviation between average scores. This raises the question that my philosophy professor, Herbert Feigl, used to ask, "How big is a difference that makes a difference?" Suppose that a measure of belief in salvation by works was standardized so that the average score for all Lutherans was 50 with a standard deviation of 10 points. Suppose you were a parochial school teacher or administrator. Would you consider it worth your continued effort if it could be demonstrated that on the average persons who attended parochial schools for 12 years would score less than one point lower than persons who did not attend? I do not believe that most of you would be interested in having such differences (of less than one-tenth of a standard deviation) reported as *significant*. Some may be interested in differences as small as a fifth or a fourth of the standard deviation. I concluded that most would find it reasonable that differences of one-third standard deviation and larger be reported as significant.

Thus on this basis, too, probability levels of .01 and preferably .001 for each test seemed best as criteria for statistical significance. With a sample as large as within this study, a probability level of .01 could lead to reporting of mean differences as small as two points (one-fifth standard deviation), and a probability level of .001 could lead to the reporting of mean differences as small as three points or approximately one-third standard deviation.

There seemed to be three alternatives: (1) stick to the conventional probability levels of .05 and .01 and run the risk, with this many hypotheses and, with this large a sample of reporting errors or trivia, or (2) arbitrarily choose a rather extremely stringent probability level of say .00001 and be assured of reporting only rather sizeable mean differences of four-tenths to half a standard deviation, but at the same time run the high risk of being much criticized, as was Johnstone, for being biased against parochial education, or (3) report differences on the basis of two probability levels (less than .01 and less than .001) and leave it to the reader to draw his own conclusions as to which differences are large enough to be of practical consequence. I chose the third alternative.

However, in this study, 78 hypotheses of no difference (null hypotheses) were being tested at a time for there were 78 scales involved. If there were one significance test for each scale, each at a probability level of .05, and each null hypothesis were actually true, then the random chance of erroneously rejecting at least one of the 78 null hypotheses would have a probability of 0.817. If each were tested at a probability level of .01, the random chance of erroneously rejecting one would be 0.543. For the .001 level for each individual test, it becomes 0.073 for the whole set of 78. Therefore using a statistical significance level of less than .01 and preferably less than .001 would seem the wisest way to avoid reporting erroneous results.

147

CHAPTER TWO NOTES

1. Since the results of analyses of variance are sensitive to unequal numbers of cases for the cells representing different combinations of levels of the independent variables, analyses were performed using several different combinations of levels for each of the variables. If results were being affected significantly by the unequal members in each cell, one might expect a very different result when the various levels of the independent variables were changed, for such changes would significantly change the number of persons in each cell of the analysis relative to the number of persons in other cells. For example, if unequal numbers of persons in the various cells were determining the results, one would expect different results depending upon whether the levels by age were $15-18$, $19-23$, $24-29$, $30-41$, $42-49$, and $50-65$; or they were $15-29$, $30-41$, $42-49$, and $50-65$; or they were $15-28$, $29-38$, $39-48$, and $49-65$. (See *A Study of Generations*, pages $21-23$, for evidence concerning these as "natural" generations identified from the data.) However, if the ame pattern of results were found across all three analyses, each using a different one of the three age groupings mentioned above, one would be on much firmer ground concluding that the results of the analysis of variance were not being determined by the unequal frequencies in the various cells. The latter proved to be the case throughout three series of analyses in which the three different groupings by age mentioned above were used and the three different parochial school attendance variables were used. The pattern of results was basically the same regarding the question of whether parochial schooling received at different times during the last 60 years seemed to consist of something different or to effect different consequences.

2. A significant interaction between age and parochial school attendance could have occurred three times for each of the 78 scales. For no scale were three significant interactions found. Two significant interactions were found for only three scales: Scale 6, Belief in the Divinity of Jesus; Scale 73, Drug Culture Orientation; and Scale 74, Personal Initiative on Church and Public Issues.

The 12 significant interactions were as follows (probability $< .01$):

Parochial School Variable

Scale No.	Scale Name	Length of Attendance	Grades Attended	Common Patterns of Attendance	Probability
6	Divinity of Jesus		X	X	.008 & .004
11	Prior Denominational Membership		X		.008
20	Supporting Others in Crises		X		.008
26	Mutual Support Among Church, Society, and Individuals			X	.005
43	Need for Religious Absolutism			X	.005

148

52	Desire for a Dependable World		X	.004
61	Image of Lutherans as Different	X		.005
73	Drug Culture Orientation	X	X	.00001 & .0001
74	Personal Initiative on Church and Public Issues	X	X	.003 & .005

3. The items specifically created to assess Gospel orientation each described a very difficult life situation in which one person had clearly sinned at the expense of others. The respondents were requested to place themselves in the position of the person who had been sinned against and were given four courses of action from which to choose. In each case, the four choices were written in such a way as to suggest dealing with the situation by democratic process, authoritarian decision, humanistic logic, or person-to-person confrontation with a desire to seek repentance and an openness to forgive in keeping with Christ's admonition in Matthew 18:15 ff. and Luke 17:3-4. However, it was noted after use of the items in data collection that what was also characteristic of the "Gospel" responses was that in all cases the course of action involved dealing with the situation on a one-to-one personal basis. Any person prone to dealing with difficult situations one-to-one only might consistently select the "Gospel" responses.

4. Scale 32, Prejudice Against the Poor and Disadvantaged, included in Table 2.3 is a sub-scale of Scale 34. Since to avoid mathematical redundancy the factor analysis upon which Tables 2.4 — 2.16 are based included only the 64 parent scales and none of the 14 sub-scales, therefore Scale 32 is not shown in Table 2.8. Likewise Scale 48 shown in Table 2.2, is not included in Table 2.15 where its parent Scale 47 is included. Scale 38 in Table 2.3 is not included in Table 2.8 where its parent Scale 37 is included.

5. In the second-order factor analysis from which, or by which, the 14 major themes running through the 64 parent scales were identified, some factors were much more cohesive than others. In fact, Factor One, The Heart of Lutheran Piety was the most cohesive, followed by Factor Two, Misbelief or Law Orientation, on down to Factor Fourteen, More Specific Gospel Orientation, which was the least cohesive. Cohesiveness is a matter of the degree to which people tend to get the same score or the same level of score on every one of the scales that cluster around the same theme. For the most cohesive factors, the scores for a given individual across all of the scales that have that factor in common are consistently at about the same level. For the weaker or less consistent scales, there is much more variation in the scores that a person will tend to get across the set of scales that have the one factor in common.

Another way of viewing the difference is to recognize that the scales that characterize a strong factor have much more in common with each other than the scales that comprise a weaker factor. This is shown also by the fact that the highest factor loadings on the strong factors are much higher on the average, whether positive or negative, than the actor loadings on the weaker factors.

149

CHAPTER THREE NOTES

1. As was mentioned in the latter portion of Chapter 2 (see also Items 721 and 722, Appendix A), the degree of their parents' church activity, as remembered in 1970 by the respondents as having been the case during their youthful years, was also positively correlated with the number of years of parochial school attended. One or both of these variables (721 or 722) could conceivably have been investigated as potential alternative "causes" of the parochially educated being different from those who never attended. However, these items (721 and 722) were not examined as possible alternative causes for the following reasons: (1) It is possible that the level of church activity reported for either mother or father, or both, could well be an effect of parochial school attendance instead of any kind of cause. We do not know how the people providing the data perceived their parents' church activity during the time that they (the respondents) were growing up. We only know how they remembered it in 1970, which represented anywhere from none to 50 years of time in which to reshape that memory. Furthermore, we have no way of knowing how accurate this perception was of the *actual* activity level of the various respondents' parents. The most that we could say about the data from Items 721 and 722 is that they represent the level of church activity for the respondent's father and mother respectively as remembered somewhere between one and 50 years after the fact. (2) The sample was too small for performing a four- or five-way analysis of variance using education, age, and length of parochial school attendance plus church activity of father and/or mother simultaneously. (3) In fact, the distributions on Items 721 and 722 were of such a nature (there were empty cells in the analysis) that even a good three-way analysis of variance using age or education, and church activity, plus length of parochial school attendance as independent variables was not possible. (As indicated in this chapter, clergy training and age were the most powerful alternative explanations for the differences observed between those who never attended and those who attended increasing numbers of years of parochial school. Therefore, the most reasonable three-way analysis, including church activity as one of the independent variables, would have included age, church activity of mother, and length of parochial school attendance as the independent variables using only the lay sample (omitting clergymen). This would have effectively controlled the respective effects of age, church activity, and clergy training as possible alternative "causes" had the sample size and distribution of the variables permitted; but they did not.)

2. The probabilities reported are for the F-tests for main effects. They indicate the probability of the five sample-group means being as different as these, due only to chance, if in reality all five groups were from the same population and were not in any way different within the entire Lutheran Church — Missouri Synod.

   Scheffé's tests were performed two-by-two on the five sample subgroups to identify which subgroups were the ones different from the rest at a probability less than .05. The ten or more probabilities that result for each scale from such subgroup contrasts using Scheffé's methods are not reported in detail. They are reflected by the heavy vertical lines separating the statistically different subgroups at Type I error-probability equal to or less than .05 for all contrasts combined. For example in table 3.16, scale 16, the heavy vertical line indicates that groups "none" and "grades 1 – 3" do not differ significantly: grade groups 4 – 6, 7 – 9. 10 – 12 do not differ significantly from each other; but both groups "none" and "1 – 3" do differ significantly from each of the grade groups 4 – 6. 7 – 9. 10 – 12 by Scheffé's tests.

CHAPTER FOUR NOTES

1. Piaget, Jean. *The Moral Judgment of the Child.* New York: Macmillan (The Free Press), 1965.
   Piaget, Jean. *Judgment and Reasoning in the Child.* London: Routledge and Kegan Paul, 1951.
   Piaget, Jean. *The Child's Conception of the World.* London: Routledge and Kegan Paul, 1951.
2. Kohlberg, Lawrence. "Development of Moral Character and Moral Ideology," in Hoffman, M. L. and L. W. (Ed.). *Review of Child Development Research.* Volume One. New York: Russell Sage Foundation, 1964.
   Kohlberg, Lawrence. "The Development of Children's Orientations Toward a Moral Order; 1. Sequence in the Development of Moral Thought." *Vita Humana* 6 (1963), 11-33b.
   Kohlberg, Lawrence. *Stages in the Development of Moral Thought and Action.* New York: Holt, Rinehart, and Winston, 1970.
3. Goldman, Ronald. *Religious Thinking from Childhood to Adolescence.* London: Routledge and Kegan Paul, 1964.
   Goldman, Ronald. *Readiness for Religion.* New York: Seabury Press, 1965.
4. For a fuller discussion of this issue and related methodological issues, see Brekke, Milo L. "Significant Evidence," Chapter 9 in Gilbert, Kent W. (ed.), *Confirmation and Education,* Volume 1, Year Books in Christian Education. Philadelphia: Fortress, 1969. That book also includes the report and recommendations of the Joint Commission on the Theology and Practice of Confirmation (LCMS, ALC and LCA). The commission's recommendations regarding a long-term confirmation ministry discourage programs concentrated in time. However, wherever there is desire to enroll previously uninvolved youth in parochial schools as part of a period of concentrated confirmation instruction, if congregations were to follow the commission's recommendation that the rite of confirmation be at about tenth grade, they would likely avoid the possible dilatorious effects of concentrated parochial education just at grades 7 – 8.
5. Fägerlind, Ingemar. "Methods of Instruction in the Subject Religion (U M Re)." *School Research Newsletter.* Stockholm: National Board of Education, Bureau L4, 1968, 2.
6. Schulz, Delbert. "Mission:Life – a New Curriculum for the Church." *Lutheran Education,* December, 1969. p. 11.
7. Strommen, Merton P.; Brekke, Milo L.; Underwager, Ralph C.; Johnson, Arthur A. *A Study of Generations.* Minneapolis: Augsburg, 1972. p. 301.
8. Watson, Goodwin. *Social Psychology: Issues and Insights.* Philadelphia and New York: J. B. Lippincott, 1966. Chapter 6.

Concordia College Library
Bronxville, NY 10708